The A-LIST WORKOUT

The

Top Celebrity Trainers
Reveal How You Can
Get a Hot Hollywood Body

ALYSSA SHAFFER

**Mc
Graw
Hill**

New York   Chicago   San Francisco   Lisbon   London   Madrid   Mexico City
Milan   New Delhi   San Juan   Seoul   Singapore   Sydney   Toronto

Library of Congress Cataloging-in-Publication Data

Shaffer, Alyssa.
    The A-list workout : top Hollywood trainers reveal how you can get a hot
Hollywood body / Alyssa Shaffer.
        p.   cm.
    Includes index.
    ISBN 0-07-146786-6 (alk. paper)
    1. Exercise.   2. Physical fitness.   3. Bodybuilding.   I. Title.

RA781.S514   2007
613.7'1—dc22   2006022979

1 2 3 4 5 6 7 8 9 10 11 12 13 14 15   DOC/DOC   0 9 8 7 6

ISBN-13: 978-0-07-146786-5
ISBN-10:   0-07-146786-6

Interior design by Monica Baziuk
Interior photographs for chapters 6, 7, 8, 9, 11, 12, and 13 by Dorit Thies
Interior photographs for chapter 10 by Chris Fanning

McGraw-Hill books are available at special quantity discounts to use as premiums and sales promotions, or for use in corporate training programs. For more information, please write to the Director of Special Sales, Professional Publishing, McGraw-Hill, Two Penn Plaza, New York, NY 10121-2298. Or contact your local bookstore.

Contents ■

PART **2**

THE WORKOUTS

Acknowledgments

MANY THANKS to my editor, Deborah Brody, for guiding this book through the process; to my agent, Linda Konner, for helping make it a reality; and to Michelle Matrisciani for opening the door. Thanks to Dorit Thies and Chris Fanning for their fantastic photos; to models Ashley Salter, AnnMarie Solo, and Cynthia Daniel for making the images look great; and to Nicole Dorsey for bringing it all together. Thanks to Liz Neporent for her guidance and feedback. And of course, thanks to Mike Alexander, Teddy Bass, Ashley Borden, Joe Dowdell, Rich and Helene Guzmán, Jeanette Jenkins, Larry Krug, Gunnar Peterson, and Christel Smith for their incredible ideas and hard work.

Thanks to all my friends and coworkers at *Fitness* magazine, especially to Liz for her enthusiasm and support, to Celeste for her fashion prowess, and to Jen for her never-ending help.

My love and appreciation to my family: To my mom and dad, for putting me on the right path and showing me what true courage means; to Grandma Dottie for teaching me the importance of finding the right words; to Andy, Jill, Cynthia, Joel, Lauren, and Jay for their encouragement. To my amazing children, Nolan and Layla, for reminding me of what's really important in life. And finally, to my husband, Scott, for his constant love, support, and companionship.

The A-LIST WORKOUT

★

★

★

★

1

GETTING STARTED

THE SUCCESS BEHIND HOLLYWOOD'S HOTTEST BODIES

YOU MAY NOT THINK you have a lot in common with some of Hollywood's biggest stars. After all, you're probably not constantly in the public spotlight, with paparazzi trailing your every move. You aren't relentlessly photographed wearing the latest fashions—or even just a tiny bikini—or the subject of tabloid headlines that scream comments about your looks or your love life. You usually don't just jet off to Paris, London, or Madrid for the weekend.

And yet . . . surprisingly, many of us do share some of the same concerns as these superstars. We all struggle with jam-packed schedules and the constant demands of others. Many of us balance work and family, struggling to fit in our own needs as well as the needs of those we love. Finding time to exercise is a constant struggle; it's sometimes easier to grab a bag of chips than to make a healthful snack. It's hard to get out of bed in the morning, and we're often exhausted by the end of the day. And whether we want to look good for the cameras or just for ourselves as we glance in the mirror, almost all of us have a constant quest for self-improvement.

Celebrities do have one big advantage over most of us: They have access to some of the world's very best personal trainers, who can help whip their bodies into shape and keep them that way. They also have the resources to devote significant expense to getting one-on-one advice and help with the latest workouts, top training tools, and nutrition plans.

Most of those amazing bodies require an incredible amount of hard work and dedication to achieve and to maintain. Some celebrities work with their trainers twice a day, morning and evening, six times a week. They have their meals specially prepared and delivered; they're given early-morning wake-up calls and are sent e-mails and text messages reminding them to get to the gym.

But take away the fancy gyms and personal chefs, and you'll find that getting into shape requires nothing more magical than good old-fashioned exercise and smart dietary choices. While many of today's most beautiful superstars are also blessed with good looks and even better genes, most have also discovered that in order to stay on top of their game and get the bodies they want, they need to find time for both of these choices, making regular exercise and a healthful diet part of their daily routine.

The primary secret to achieving a fit, sexy, healthy body is this: dedication. The best bodies in Hollywood stay dedicated to a healthy eating plan and consistent in their exercise habits, meaning they put in time with regular strength and cardiovascular workouts. At the end of the day, that is what gets lasting results.

And what results they are! Beyoncé's sexy silhouette, Jennifer Aniston's sculpted arms, Jessica Simpson's long, lean legs, and Madonna's ageless physique have become the stuff of legend. Day after day, magazines, newspapers, and the Internet treat us to images of some of Hollywood's most amazing bodies. Headlines shriek of "Slim-Down Special" and "20 Best Body Makeovers," all profiling the shape-up secrets of the stars. It's in large part credit to the workout and lifestyle regimens of their trainers that they can tout their sleek muscles and eye-popping curves.

The good news is this: you can get the same amazing results, without having to dedicate your life to the gym or resigning yourself to eat celery and carrots 24/7. Some of the top trainers in Hollywood and New York have come together to give you their favorite exercise plans and tips for getting your dream body. They have all worked with some of the biggest names in the business, helping them get slim, trim, and sculpted for their lives before the cameras and back home. These trainers help them reach their fitness goals and to find time to exercise in even the busiest schedules. They keep the stars motivated to stay in shape and entice them back for more with winning strategies, cutting-edge techniques, and a passion for fitness.

Although it's their star clients who make the headlines, these trainers have more than A-list celebrities on their customer rosters. They don't just work with the rich and successful. Their advice is also geared to "regular folks" who simply want to shed a few extra pounds, develop more endurance, or feel better about themselves.

The plans outlined in this book will help you reach your goals, whether you simply want to start an exercise program, reshape your entire body, blast away a specific trouble zone, or lose weight. Although these goals all require a certain amount of time exercising, you won't have to spend hours each day working up a sweat. And while you can do the program in the gym, you can also follow along on your own at home. As for a healthful diet, we've created a week's worth of menu plans that won't make you feel deprived.

Of course, everyone's body is different, and no one can promise you that you'll instantly morph into supermodel shape. What we can promise you is this: If you make a commitment to regular exercise and diet, you will see changes in your body for the better. You may never get to a size 2 (and likely don't have to come close to that to reach your ideal weight), but you will make improvements in your health and build lean, sexy muscles while blasting fat and firming up everywhere.

The goal of *The A-List Workout* is not simply to present a look at how some of the sexiest members of the Hollywood elite keep their amazing physiques. It's to help you improve your fitness by shaping up and slimming down in the privacy of home or at the gym, based on the knowledge of some of the world's most influential fitness experts. If you're just getting started with an exercise plan, welcome! You'll find beginner-friendly options throughout the book to help you get started on a lifetime of healthy habits. If you've already committed yourself to an exercise program and are looking to shake things up, you've come to the right place: many of the exercises given in this book are unique and challenging enough to get results you never thought possible.

Let's meet the A-List trainers who will help you on this incredible journey:

Mike Alexander was born and raised in Dallas. He earned a degree in health/fitness at Baylor University and worked as a personal trainer in Dallas after graduation. In the fall of 2003, he moved to Los Angeles, where he opened MADFit (Mike Alexander Designed Fitness) early in 2006. He has a large celebrity clientele, including Jessica Simpson, Ashlee Simpson, and singers Natalie Maines and Emily Robison of the Dixie Chicks.

A former professional dancer, trainer **Teddy Bass** boasts a client list that includes Lucy Liu, Paris Hilton, and Christina Applegate, plus numerous other Hollywood celebs and executives. Teddy's workouts marry traditional strength-training exercises with Pilates-based moves that focus on improving core stability, posture, and alignment. He is a certified trainer from the American Council on Exercise (ACE) and also holds a certification from Future Fit. He trains clients at The Gym Private Fitness in Los Angeles. He is a graduate of the University of North Carolina at Greensboro.

Ashley Borden is a Los Angeles–based fitness and lifestyle consultant who has worked with numerous Hollywood celebrities, including Christina Aguilera, Mandy Moore, Tori Spelling, and Lauren Graham. A Nike Fitness Professional, she also recently began a partnership with the luxurious, five-star Four Seasons Resort in Punta Mita, Mexico, where she offers exclusive, personalized fitness retreats. Her unique approach to fitness can be attributed to her transformation of her own personal struggles into a positive philosophy and dynamic training program.

Personal trainer and strength coach **Joe Dowdell** has used his motivating teaching style and unique expertise to transform a clientele that includes stars of television and film, musicians, pro athletes, CEOs, and top fashion models from around the world, including Claire Danes, Molly Sims, Anne Hathaway, and several *Sports Illustrated* swimsuit and Victoria's Secret models—an association reflecting his own former career in front of the camera. He is the founder and co-owner of Peak Performance Strength & Conditioning Center, a 10,000-square-foot loft in New York City, which admits only training clients. Over the past decade, Joe has earned a dozen top fitness certifications in the field, including Certified Strength and Conditioning Specialist from the National Strength and Conditioning Association (NSCA), Certified Personal Trainer from the National Academy of Sports Medicine (NASM), and Certified Personal Trainer from the American Council on Exercise (ACE). He serves on the advisory board of *Fitness* magazine and is currently working on his own book, *The Model You,* which will be geared toward women and strength training.

Rich Edward Guzmán and **Helene Chimbidis Guzmán** cofounded Los Angeles Resourceful Onsite X-training (L.A. R.O.X.) in 1999. The facility serves a broad spectrum of athletes, film and television industry members, and numerous other clients. Rich is a certified personal fitness coach and nutritionist with a B.A. from Pomona College; Helene is a certified personal fitness coach and the managing director of L.A. R.O.X. Together they have trained dozens of celebrities, including Minnie Driver, Hilary Swank, Sheryl Crow, Selma Blair, Joaquin Phoenix, Christian Slater, and Giovanni Ribisi.

Jeanette Jenkins is founder and president of The Hollywood Trainer (thehollywoodtrainer.com) and a Nike Elite Athlete. Her client rosters include well-known actors, professional athletes, swimsuit models, and Hollywood executives, including Queen Latifah, Taryn Manning, Tom Arnold, and Ty Law. The NFL's Terrell Owens describes Jeanette as being "high energy, passionate, and knowledgeable." "Jeanette knows how to draw you in and keep you motivated," says Owens. She also teaches group classes at some of L.A.'s top fitness clubs. She is a resident expert on the Food Network's weight loss show "Weighing In," the official spokesperson for the BET Foundation's "A Healthy BET" campaign, and one of the directors for the End Childhood Obesity nonprofit organization. She studied human kinetics at the University of Ottawa, Canada, and has earned over seventeen international certifications in various methods of training.

Larry Krug holds a bachelor's degree in exercise physiology and a master's degree in nutrition. He specializes in metabolic research and is a Certified Nutrition Specialist by the American College of Nutrition. Larry has trained, coached, and counseled such stars as Estella Warren, Anabeth Gish, Donatella Versace, Jeanne Tripplehorn, Seal, Monet Mazur, and Jessica Capshaw. He is the coauthor of *Get Fit in a Crunch* and is the nutrition spokesperson for Crunch Fitness International and the former celebrity nutritionist for VH1's "Flab to Fab" fitness series. He is the founder of eatwize.com, a lifestyle and weight loss consulting company.

Gunnar Peterson is a Beverly Hills–based trainer whose clients have included Jennifer Lopez, Angelina Jolie, Penelope Cruz, Debra Messing, and Mary J. Blige—plus numerous other film and television celebrities and professional athletes from the NBA, NFL, NHL, USTA, and boxing. Gunnar has a private facility and is a founding partner of Outside Shot, a fitness product development company. He is the creator of the Core Secrets DVD series and the author of *The Workout.* Gunnar is widely recognized for his expertise in functional training and innovative fitness techniques. He is a Certified Strength and Conditioning Specialist (CSCS) by the National Strength and Conditioning Association and is certified by the American Council on Exercise. He is a contributing editor to *Muscle & Fitness* magazine and serves on the advisory board of *Fitness* magazine. Gunnar received his B.A. from Duke University.

South Africa–born **Christel Smith** studied ballet, tap, flamenco, and jazz dance for fifteen years and is a national-level aerobics championships medal holder. She is also a long-distance runner and completed the grueling fifty-six-mile Comrades ultra-marathon. She has used her dance and choreography background to train such clients as Uma Thurman, Daryl Hannah, and Julia Ormond. Christel has appeared in numerous South African television shows and films. She is a contributing writer to various websites and publications and writes monthly for the *Brentwood News.* She traveled with cast members to China to train them for the Quentin Tarantino film *Kill Bill.*

2

EVERY BODY STARTS SOMEWHERE

THERE'S NO BIGGER EVENT in Hollywood than the Academy Awards. Weeks and even months in advance, the biggest names in the business begin the process of primping and preening to get set before the eyes of the world. Hairstyles are changed, gowns are carefully considered, and trainers pump up workouts with the goal of helping their clients look their sleekest and sexiest before they hit the red carpet.

There's always an instant wow factor when you see an amazing body take a turn before the cameras. Sculpted arms, flat abs, lean legs, and a firm butt make headlines and magazine spreads for months to come. Online chat rooms and offices alike buzz with talk of who looked the best, whose body really impressed—and who ended up looking like a dud.

SETTING A GOAL

You may never have to step out of a limo and into the gaze of millions of viewers across the globe, but it's likely you've had your own event to train for, be it a wedding, high school reunion, or even just a beach vacation. In fact, having a goal, or even a series of short-term goals, is a great way to keep motivated to work out and establish some healthy lifestyle patterns that will last for years to come.

Many of the celeb clients who have come to the trainers in this book do so because they have their own goals. Usually, it's working on a project with specific time constraints, like getting ready to play an action star or athlete in a major movie. Some have goals that are more like yours; they want more energy, especially with the demands of a busy schedule. A few smoke and want to quit. And most simply want to look their best, both for themselves and for their public images.

"Many of our celebrity clients are working on projects like a movie or tour," explains Helene Guzmán, co-owner of L.A. R.O.X. Fitness. "But even when they're not preparing for a work-related event, we try to keep them on track with other things, like training for a triathlon. It keeps them motivated to have a specific goal in mind."

One of the most important ideas in having a goal is to set a deadline for yourself. The plans outlined in this book give you twelve weeks to reach your goals, though you will likely start to see results in just a quarter of that time. Change will not come overnight, but by establishing a nutritious diet and regular exercise early on, you'll be setting yourself up for a lifetime of healthy habits.

Another key part of goal setting is to make sure your plans are realistic. You will not drop six dress sizes in the course of the plan; in many cases, it's not something you should ever need to do. Crash diets, as you probably know, don't deliver lasting results. Most nutrition experts recommend losing about one pound a week. Getting yourself to a healthy weight—and maybe falling one or two clothing sizes in the course of the program—should be your end goal for the next three months.

And remember that even celebrities don't think they have a "perfect body." Some of the biggest stars still nitpick about their own appearances. Most importantly, all of us are somewhat limited by our own genetic makeup. Most of us simply aren't born with the ability to get a body like Cameron Diaz's or Nicole Kidman's—but you may be more likely to develop sleek curves like Halle Berry's or Jennifer Lopez's.

"You have to manage your expectations," says trainer Gunnar Peterson. "Eighty-five percent of women, when asked to draw their own silhouette, draw their lower extremities 30 percent bigger than they are in real life. They see themselves a certain way, and it's not always realistic."

Also important is to make your goals specific. "I want to lose weight" can be vague and open ended, but "I want to drop ten pounds" gives you real numbers to shoot for. Replace "I just want to look better" with something more tangible, like "I want to firm up my legs and butt." Even a goal like running your first 5K from start to finish or hiking up a favorite trail can give you confidence and boost your motivation.

Finally, keep your goals going from one to the next. Set smaller goals, like fitting into a new swimsuit for a beach party that's coming up in one month or completing a charity 5K race taking place in a few weeks, as a way to stay on top of your program. Put in the time, say the experts, and you'll begin to see a change for the better.

"Exercise is all about consistency," says Guzmán. "We try to make sure our clients stay consistent by tailoring a program that suits their schedule. If they are more into exercising in the A.M., we get them here in the early part of the day. If they skip a workout, we encourage them to simply make it to the next one, so the whole week is not ruined because of one bad day."

We've prepared this book to help you reach some very specific goals with our detailed workout plans, based on the routines top trainers give their own celebrity clientele. Choose what you want based not only on your desires, but also on where you may need improvement. If you're new to fitness or returning

$\mathcal{S}$ETTING GOALS

Do you have other goals that you'd like to achieve? Write down your short-term goals for the next few weeks and months. They'll become more realistic (and more of a motivation) when they're in front of you in black and white.

My Overall Goal _____

_____

One month from now, I want to be able to: _____

_____

Three months from now, I want to be able to: _____

_____

One year from now, I would like to: _____

_____

after a long layoff and your goal is to get fit and healthy, look to the details of the beginner's program on page 46. If you're more experienced with exercise and want to get a lean, sculpted body, choose the total-body tone-up plan on page 50. If you're interested in targeting a specific trouble zone, check out the ab-flattening plan (page 60), the upper-body sculpting plan (page 54), or the bottom-boosting plan (page 57). And if weight loss is your primary goal, turn to the plan detailed on pages 64–66.

FITTING IT IN

We all have busy days. Most of us feel jam-packed from the moment the alarm goes off in the morning to the time our head hits the pillow again at night. Celebs often face the same demanding days. "The biggest challenge for celebrities is the same as the rest of us—not enough time during the day," says trainer Ashley Borden, who worked with singer Christina Aguilera for almost three years. "Her schedule was a nightmare—sometimes we had to go to the gym at 11 P.M. just to fit in a workout."

That may be extreme, but the idea, says Borden, is that you have to be flexible with your exercise routine to make it work for you. Can't get out of the house in the morning because you have to get your kids off to school? Set the alarm a half hour earlier than usual, and do the routine at home. Busy day at the office? Sneak in a lunchtime workout, or hit the gym on your way home before you even set foot back in your house or apartment. "I recommend my clients work out in the morning, before the demands of the day fit in, and because it helps you to start the day out on the right foot," says Peterson. "But you need to do what works best for you and your schedule."

Remember, too, that you can always divide your workouts into more frequent, shorter sessions. If you're scheduled to do thirty minutes of cardio but don't have a full half hour at any one point, do a fifteen-minute workout in the morning and another fifteen minutes at night. Research has shown you'll still get the same overall benefits from splitting it into two or more parts.

"Plan your workouts into your daily routine," says trainer Christel Smith. "It should be a way of life, something you automatically do, like sleeping or eating." If you have a date or are meeting a friend after work but haven't yet gotten to the gym to fit in your workout, push your plans back an hour, and squeeze in a short workout session. "Make exercise as important as some of your other plans, and magic will happen! You'll start to see that you just can't get by without wanting to work out on a regular basis," says Smith.

BEST WAYS TO BUST COMMON WORKOUT EXCUSES

The excuse: "I'm too busy."

The solution: Write down your day. Even the busiest Hollywood executives find time to squeeze in a workout. Sure, it might be long before the sun rises, but the fact remains that if an actress who shoots twelve hours a day has time to work out, so do you. Map out your week, from start to finish, and then look for holes in your schedule. If you can find even twenty spare minutes a day, you have enough time to at least get in some form of fitness.

The excuse: "I'm exhausted."

The solution: Just do it. Even just a few minutes of exercise itself can be a big boost. Try going for a walk or just doing a few small sets of strength moves. After a few minutes, you'll probably start to perk up and feel motivated to do more.

The excuse: "I'm battling an injury."

The solution: Work what you can. Cross-training can go a long way toward helping you recover from a current ache or pain and even prevent future problems. If you've got a sore knee or ankle, try a low-impact move like swimming or walking. If you're battling a shoulder injury or back pain, hop onto a stationary or recumbent bicycle. If you've got a muscle injury, avoid the problem area, but mind the rest of your body.

The excuse: "I don't have the money."

The solution: Be creative. You don't have to join a gym to reap the benefits of fitness. Inexpensive workout tools like dumbbells, stability balls, and jump ropes can be bought new or used online though sites like eBay and Craigslist. Even your body weight or some common household items like milk jugs or water bottles can be used for resistance for a bare-bones workout.

The excuse: "I'm not in good enough shape."

Continued

> **The solution:** There's almost never a point where you are so out of shape that you can't begin to exercise. Maybe you won't be diving into a triathlon in the near future, but even just a short walk around the block can be a realistic starting point—and a building block for further action.
>
> **The excuse:** "It's too painful!"
>
> **The solution:** That mild discomfort you may feel when you lift a weight, stretch a muscle, or break a sweat is your body's way of telling you you're getting to work. And since no great thing was ever accomplished without a little hard work along the way, think of this as an opportunity to create a better, healthier you.

ESSENTIALS OF A FIT BODY

Getting a body like Jennifer Garner's might be your initial workout motivation, but what keeps you staying committed to exercise is the way your body *feels*. "Your primary motivation should really be establishing a better quality of life," says Peterson. "Improve your health and daily function; then worry about your appearance."

The point is that while we all want to look our best, one of the best payoffs of regular exercise is how it makes you feel. "I have clients who say one of the biggest benefits they've gotten from working out is just the amount of energy they have in their day," says Smith.

The health benefits of fitness are really staggering. Exercise itself is a veritable fountain of youth. Working out just an hour a day can be better than almost any pill when it comes to reducing your risk of heart disease or stroke. Study after study has found that regular exercise can greatly lower your chances of developing certain cancers like breast, colon, and ovarian cancer. One major research project found that those who are at risk for type 2 diabetes (the most common type of the disease in the United States) slashed their odds by nearly half when they followed a regular exercise program.

Exercise also is just as good for your mind as for your body. Increasingly, researchers are finding that regular exercise can help fight depression, anxiety, and stress. One recent study found that being active can stimulate brain cell growth and lower the risk of Alzheimer's disease. Best of all, regular exercise can add years to your life: one study found that physically active people live an average of three and a half years longer than those who are sedentary.

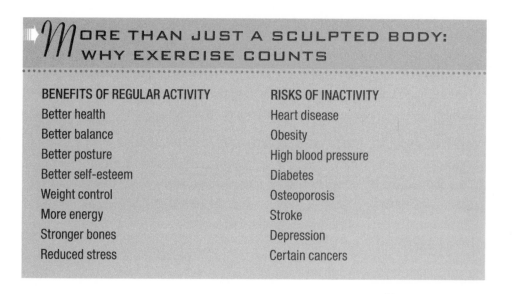

MORE THAN JUST A SCULPTED BODY: WHY EXERCISE COUNTS

BENEFITS OF REGULAR ACTIVITY	RISKS OF INACTIVITY
Better health	Heart disease
Better balance	Obesity
Better posture	High blood pressure
Better self-esteem	Diabetes
Weight control	Osteoporosis
More energy	Stroke
Stronger bones	Depression
Reduced stress	Certain cancers

THREE PILLARS OF FITNESS

Most forms of exercise are divided into one of three main types: strength, cardiovascular, and flexibility. All successful programs should include each of these elements, with the amounts varying depending on your makeup and goals. Some of us can get away with less flexibility training than others; if weight loss is your primary goal, you'll need to amp up the cardio. To get a lean, muscular body, strength training itself is the key. But all of these exercise forms work together to help you get your dream body.

Some trainers also include a fourth element, balance, in their programs. "Adding a balance challenge to a workout, like standing on one leg or using a device like a wobble board, is a more functional way to get fit," explains Peterson. "It's a lot more like the challenges you face in daily life." If you slip going down the stairs or stepping off a curb, having better balance can help you avoid a fall—and reduce your risk of a sprained ankle or worse. Several of the work-outs in this book incorporate balance-type drills that will carry over to the daily demands of life.

THE EXPERTS RECOMMEND . . .

How much exercise do you need to reach your goals? You'll hear many different answers from many different people, but at a minimum, try following the guidelines put forth by the American College of Sports Medicine, the leading group of fitness experts in the United States. Here is their *minimum* prescription for maintaining a fit, healthy body:

CARDIOVASCULAR FITNESS (AEROBIC ACTIVITY)
Twenty to sixty minutes of moderate to intense aerobic activity, three to five days a week. Recommended activities include walking, hiking, running, jogging, cycling, cross-country skiing, aerobic dance or group exercise, jumping rope, rowing, stair climbing, swimming, skating, and other options that use large muscle groups and can be maintained continuously.

MUSCULAR STRENGTH AND ENDURANCE
One to three sets of eight to twelve repetitions for eight to ten exercises that condition the major muscle groups; two to three days a week.

FLEXIBILITY TRAINING
Incorporate flexibility exercises into an overall fitness program, stretching the major muscle groups, at least two to three days a week.

OVERALL CALORIC EXPENDITURE
Burn 700 to 2,000 or more calories of effort per week.

Many significant health benefits can be achieved simply by going from a sedentary state to some physical activity. Programs involving higher intensities, frequency, and dura-tion provide additional benefits. If you're just starting an exercise program, it's OK to stay on the lower end, especially to see some basic health benefits. But to achieve more pronounced changes in body composition or achieve certain fitness goals, you need to incorporate more physical activity into your lifestyle.

A HEALTHY HEART AND MORE: BENEFITS OF CARDIOVASCULAR FITNESS

You know working up a sweat is good for your heart. In fact, hundreds of studies have shown aerobic activity will reduce the risk of heart disease, improve blood cholesterol and triglyceride levels, and improve heart function. Moreover, weight-bearing cardio workouts like walking or running can help build stronger bones and reduce the risk of osteoporosis, boost mental health, lower the odds of developing diabetes and other chronic ailments, and even stimulate brain cell growth and lower the risk of Alzheimer's disease. And you don't have to be training for a marathon to get these benefits. One eight-year study of thirteen thousand people found that those who walked just thirty minutes a day had a significantly lower risk of premature death than those who rarely exercised.

For anyone interested in weight loss, cardiovascular exercise is the key. After all, to drop pounds, you need to expend more energy than you consume, and one of the fastest ways to do this is through aerobic activity. "It comes down to calories in, calories out," says trainer Jeanette Jenkins. "The more energy you burn off through exercise, the more you will be able to tip the balance so you're burning more calories than you take in."

Any aerobic activity that elevates your heart rate can help you burn fat and lose weight. Cardio exercise is also the key to helping reduce your overall body fat, which plays an important role when it comes to targeting specific spots like the legs and butt. To zap your trouble zones, you need to do a combination of cardiovascular exercise to burn unwanted body fat all over plus strength training to tone these muscle groups.

We'll talk more about the different types of cardio exercise in Chapter 12, but the important thing is to choose an activity you enjoy doing. If you like to walk, go for an evening power stroll; if sports are your thing, find a regular pickup game in your neighborhood or join a recreational league. And don't forget that in addition to lacing up your sneakers, you can also burn additional calories throughout the day just through small changes in your activity level. Take the stairs instead of the elevator, walk to run an errand instead of driving, and do some additional chores around the house. Even these small steps can burn up to a few hundred extra calories by the end of the week.

HOW MANY CALORIES WILL I BURN IN ONE HOUR?

	120 LB.	140 LB.	160 LB.	180 LB.
Aerobics (low-impact)	360	420	480	540
Aerobics (high-impact)	504	588	672	756
Ballroom dancing	324	378	432	486
Bicycling: 12–13.9 mph	576	672	768	864
14–15.9 mph	720	840	960	1,080
16–19 mph	864	1,008	1,152	1,296
Bicycling, stationary: moderate pace	504	588	672	756
vigorous pace	756	882	1,008	1,134
Boxing (punching bag)	432	504	576	648
Calisthenics (vigorous)	576	672	768	864
Circuit training	576	672	768	864
Cleaning house	216	252	288	324
Cross-country ski machine	504	588	672	756
Dancing (fast, ballet)	346	403	461	518
Elliptical trainer	518	605	691	778
Golf: using cart	252	294	336	378
walking, pulling clubs	310	361	413	464
Hiking cross country	432	504	576	648
Ice-skating	504	588	672	756
In-line skating	900	1,050	1,200	1,350
Jumping rope	720	840	960	1,080
Kickboxing/martial arts	720	840	960	1,080
Playing with kids	288	336	384	432
Rowing: moderate	504	588	672	756
vigorous	612	714	816	918
Running: 12 min./mi.	576	672	768	864
10 min./mi.	720	840	960	1,080
9 min./mi.	792	924	1,056	1,188
8.5 min./mi.	828	966	1,104	1,242
7 min./mi.	1,008	1,176	1,344	1,512

Continued

	120 LB.	140 LB.	160 LB.	180 LB.
Snowshoeing	576	672	768	864
Softball	360	420	480	540
Step aerobics	720	840	960	1,080
Strength training: light	216	252	288	324
vigorous	432	504	576	648
Swimming laps: moderate	576	672	768	864
vigorous	720	840	960	1,080
Tennis: singles	576	672	768	864
doubles	360	420	480	540
Walking: 20 min./mi.	238	277	317	356
17 min./mi.	274	319	365	410
15 min./mi.	360	420	480	540
13 min./mi.	454	529	605	680
Water aerobics	288	336	384	432
Yoga (hatha)	180	210	240	270

Source: Adapted from Ainsworth et al. "Compendium of Physical Activities: An Update of Activity Codes and MET Intensities," *Medicine & Science in Sports & Exercise*, September 2000.

MIND YOUR MUSCLES: WHY EVERYONE NEEDS STRENGTH TRAINING

Lifting weights does more than build strong, sexy muscles, although for many of us, that's the main motivator to picking up a dumbbell. Strength training also has myriad benefits, from reducing blood pressure to lowering LDL ("bad") cholesterol and elevating HDL ("good") cholesterol levels. Weight training may also improve the way the body processes sugar, which may reduce the risk of diabetes. It can help reduce the incidence of osteoarthritis, an often-painful joint condition that primarily strikes older adults. And it can strengthen bones, muscle, and connective tissue, decreasing your risk of injury in other activities while preventing osteoporosis later in life. Finally, being strong means making certain daily activities, from carrying groceries to lifting your children, easier and more manageable.

Strength training is also the key to losing weight and preventing weight gain by staving off the loss of muscle mass that often occurs with age. Most adults lose about one-half pound of muscle each year beginning at age 20. Since muscle mass is a very metabolically active tissue, it takes energy to maintain even at rest, and it plays an important part in the total number of calories you burn each day. Some experts estimate you'll burn up to fifty extra calories a day for each pound of muscle you add to your physique.

When you're first starting a strength-training program, progress seems to come very quickly. Many beginning exercisers show immediate gains in strength and muscle tone. However, after a few weeks, strength improvements begin to slow. To stay motivated and avoid reaching a plateau, mix it up by trying new exercises or using new equipment every three to four weeks. Not only will you avoid burnout, you'll challenge your muscles in new ways and see better results.

⟩ *F*IT FACT: WHICH BODY PART SHOWS RESULTS THE FASTEST?

According to a recent study, upper-body muscles like the biceps, triceps, and chest increase in size significantly faster than the hamstrings and quadriceps.

STAYING FLEXIBLE: WHY STRETCH?

In the past few years, researchers have begun to rethink flexibility training, usually considered the third pillar in achieving good fitness, along with strength and cardiovascular activities. Surprisingly, new studies have shown that some long-held conceptions about stretching (that it decreases injury and improves performance) may, in fact, be false. One major study found that stretching before a workout failed to reduce the rate of injury among 1,500 participants; others have found that stretching before a workout may even inhibit performance and increase injury risk.

So why stretch at all? More research does support the idea that increasing flexibility will help with balance, coordination, posture, and "functional fitness," or the fitness that you use in everyday life, like stepping down off a curb or carrying heavy bags. As we age, flexibility can help prevent falls and fractures, and an improved range of motion becomes especially important for maintaining daily activity levels.

The controversy about stretching is really twofold: the problems seem to arise with when and how you stretch. Many experts now agree that static stretching (the kind where you reach forward and hold for twenty to thirty seconds) *before* exercise may not produce the best results. Instead, they recommend doing an active warm-up of exercises like arm circles or knee-ups (bringing your knees toward your chest) for three to five minutes to get your joints and muscles loose and limber. Save the stretching for *after* your workout, when your muscles are already warm and pliable. Static stretching may be OK, but for a better option, try trainer Ashley Borden's special active-isolated stretches in Chapter 13.

BALANCING ACT

Balance training is all the buzz among top trainers and their clientele. As mentioned before, balance is perhaps the most practical aspect of fitness that you can improve. Not only will good balance help you with the other elements of fitness, it will improve your life dramatically, especially as you age. If you play any sport, balance is vital in helping you change direction or react quickly, whether to a tennis ball bouncing over the net or a mogul run down a mountain. Better balance will help you get a more effective workout, because you'll be able to work harder in certain strength moves or maintain your form when doing an aerobic activity like running or cycling. If you do sustain an injury, balance training can be crucial in your rehabilitation, especially for injuries like ankle sprains and even knee, hip, or spine injuries. And practicing better balance will help you return to daily activity more quickly.

Balance is also one of the areas where you can see the fastest gains. Just a few minutes of balance training—even doing something as simple as standing on one leg for a minute or two—can produce a dramatic improvement.

YOUR BODY OF WORK

B Y NOW, HOPEFULLY, you've caught the fitness bug and are anxious to get going on your new program. But before you dive in, it's important to take a few minutes to figure out your starting point.

All of the trainers in this book kick off their clients' programs by asking some very important questions and then establishing a starting point by determining each client's current fitness levels and body composition (ratio of fat to lean muscle mass). Knowing what you have to lose in terms of body fat (if that is one of your primary goals), what you are capable of doing, and what steps you need to take to reach your goals is crucial for creating a successful exercise strategy.

A CLEAN BILL OF HEALTH

First off, before you even start to think about working up a sweat, it's a good idea to check with your doctor to make sure you're not at risk for any conditions that can limit your participation. Some trainers give their clients a physical activity questionnaire that suggests more specific guidance about whether you need to alert your health care professional or trainer. Before you begin your program, answer the questions provided on the next page. The questionnaire is primarily geared for participants ages 15 to 69 who are stepping up their activity levels; if you're over 69 and are not used to being very active, check with your doctor regardless of your answers to the questions.

PHYSICAL ACTIVITY QUESTIONNAIRE

1. Has your doctor ever informed you that you have a heart condition? _____ Yes _____No
2. Do you feel pain in your chest when you do physical activity? _____ Yes _____No
3. In the past month, have you had chest pain when you were not doing physical activity? _____ Yes _____No
4. Do you ever lose your balance because of dizziness or lost consciousness? _____ Yes _____No
5. Do you have a bone or joint problem (such as a back, knee, or hip injury) that could be aggravated by a change in physical activity? _____ Yes _____No
6. Are you currently taking any medications for blood pressure or a heart condition? _____ Yes _____No
7. Do you now or have you ever smoked? _____ Yes _____No
8. Do you currently have any other reasons why you should not be physically active? _____ Yes _____No

If you answered Yes to any of these questions, consult your doctor before starting any exercise program.

TAKING MEASUREMENT

In addition to the change in your fitness level, you can expect your body composition to change. Some trainers swear by the scale; others would rather monitor things like body fat and circumference. Trainers have a few tools to help their clients set realistic goals when it comes to body composition and weight loss. Remember, though, that no number will tell you the whole story about your fitness level. Consider all of the numbers given—your weight, body mass index (BMI), body fat percentage and waist-to-hip ratio—when determining your goals and starting point.

To begin, figure out where you fit in when it comes to setting a healthy weight goal. Numbers on the scale can give you a starting point, but a better way to tell is to use the BMI, which considers both height and weight in determining the norm. A scale will tell you only how much you weigh, not how much of your weight is fat and how much is muscle. BMI approximates both of these through a set formula. BMI falls into one of four categories: underweight, normal, overweight, or obese.

If your BMI is below 18.5, you are underweight. A BMI between 18.5 and 24.9 is considered normal, or healthy. A range of 25.0 and 29.9 is overweight, and any number above 30 is classified as obese.

However, one shortcoming of the BMI is that it doesn't bring body fat into the equation. Someone with the chiseled muscles of Hugh Jackman might have the same BMI as the plumper Jack Black, but a much bigger difference in the percentages of body fat and lean muscle mass. Pound for pound, muscle takes up much less space than fat. If you place a pound of muscle next to a pound of fat, the muscle would be 22 percent smaller. That's why two people of the same weight can wear two different sizes of clothing.

BODY MASS INDEX (BMI)

BMI	19	20	21	22	23	24	25	26	27	28	29	30	31	32	33	34	35
HEIGHT	WEIGHT (IN POUNDS)																
4'10" (58")	91	96	100	105	110	115	119	124	129	134	138	143	148	153	158	162	167
4'11" (59")	94	99	104	109	114	119	124	128	133	138	143	148	153	158	163	168	173
5'0" (60")	97	102	107	112	118	123	128	133	138	143	148	153	158	163	168	174	179
5'1" (61")	100	106	111	116	122	127	132	137	143	148	153	158	164	169	174	180	185
5'2" (62")	104	109	115	120	126	131	136	142	147	153	158	164	169	175	180	186	191
5'3" (63")	107	113	118	124	130	135	141	146	152	158	163	169	175	180	186	191	197
5'4" (64")	110	116	122	128	134	140	145	151	157	163	169	174	180	186	192	197	204
5'5" (65")	114	120	126	132	138	144	150	156	162	168	174	180	186	192	198	204	210
5'6" (66")	118	124	130	136	142	148	155	161	167	173	179	186	192	198	204	210	216
5'7" (67")	121	127	134	140	146	153	159	166	172	178	185	191	198	204	211	217	223
5'8" (68")	125	131	138	144	151	158	164	171	177	184	190	197	203	210	216	223	230
5'9" (69")	128	135	142	149	155	162	169	176	182	189	196	203	209	216	223	230	236
5'10" (70")	132	139	146	153	160	167	174	181	188	195	202	209	216	222	229	236	243
5'11" (71")	136	143	150	157	165	172	179	186	193	200	208	215	222	229	236	243	250
6'0" (72")	140	147	154	162	169	177	184	191	199	206	213	221	228	235	242	250	258
6'1" (73")	144	151	159	166	174	182	189	197	204	212	219	227	235	242	250	257	265
6'2" (74")	148	155	163	171	179	186	194	202	210	218	225	233	241	249	256	264	272
6'3" (75")	152	160	168	176	184	192	200	208	216	224	232	240	248	256	264	272	279

Source: National Institutes of Health (NIH), National Heart, Lung, and Blood Institute, *Clinical Guidelines on the Identification, Evaluation, and Treatment of Overweight and Obesity in Adults: Evidence Report,* NIH Publication 98-4083 (September 1998).

BODY MEASUREMENTS

If you work with a trainer directly, he or she will probably help you find your body fat percentage through an electronic device called a bioelectrical impedance scale, which uses electrical currents to determine fat levels, or by measuring certain areas on your body (skin folds) with special calipers. But these devices are either expensive or too cumbersome to use by yourself. An easier method to gauge your own body fat loss as you begin an exercise program is to take measurements of some key areas, using a simple tape measure, and then recheck your progress every few weeks.

Try to take your measurements first thing in the morning, before you get dressed. The tape measure should feel snug but not so tight that it pulls or constricts you. Measure the following areas:

- Waist at belly button
- Waist about one inch above belly button
- Thigh at widest point
- Hips at widest point

Write down these measurements, and then take new measurements at weeks 5 and 9 and at the end of week 12.

	Week 1	Week 5	Week 9	Week 12
Waist at belly button	_____	_____	_____	_____
Waist above belly button	_____	_____	_____	_____
Right thigh	_____	_____	_____	_____
Left thigh	_____	_____	_____	_____
Hips	_____	_____	_____	_____

WAIST-TO-HIP RATIO

Finally, one other tool you can use to determine whether or not you need to shed some extra pounds is to calculate your waist-to-hip ratio. This measurement divides the girth of your waist by the girth of your hips. Because the fat that accumulates around the abdominals is associated with such conditions as

ℬODY FAT: WHAT'S THE RIGHT AMOUNT?

If you have access to a scale or device that measures body fat, you can use the following numbers as a guide to determine optimum levels.

	ESSENTIAL FAT	ATHLETIC	FIT	ACCEPTABLE	OBESE
Women	10%–12%	14%–20%	21%–24%	25%–31%	32%+
Men	2%–4%	6%–13%	14%–17%	18%–24%	25%+

Source: Richard J. Siebert and Richard T. Cotton, *American Council on Exercise Personal Trainer Manual* (San Diego: American Council on Exercise, 1996), 192.

heart disease, high blood pressure, and diabetes, it's also a simple way to see whether you are at risk for weight-related health conditions.

1. Stand with your stomach relaxed. Using a simple tape measure, find the narrowest point at your waist, and measure it.

   Waist measurement: _____

2. Next, find the widest point of your hips and buttocks, and measure it.

   Hip measurement: _____

3. Divide the results from step 1 by the results of step 2. This is your waist-to-hip ratio (WHR).

   Waist measurement/hip measurement = _____

   Example:
   Waist measurement: 28 inches
   Hip measurement: 35 inches
   28/35 = 0.80

Most women should aim for a WHR of less than 0.80; men should aim for a WHR of less than 0.90.

	Excellent	Good	Average	High	Very High
Women	< 0.75	0.75–0.80	0.81–0.85	0.86–0.90	> 0.90
Men	< 0.85	0.86–0.90	0.91–0.95	0.96–1.00	> 1.00

FINDING YOUR FITNESS BASELINE

You may have been able to run a seven-minute mile in high school or bench your body weight a decade ago, but a lot can change over the course of a few years. More important, your current state can tell you a lot about where you are in terms of your fitness level and how much you need to improve. Trainers often administer certain standardized tests to help their clients find a baseline from which to build.

The following tests were designed to measure some of the fundamental areas of fitness, including aerobic endurance, strength, and flexibility. Take them before you begin the program, and then track your progress by retaking them at weeks 5 and 9 and at the end of week 12. You should see improvements across the board. If you're lagging behind in any area, try adding an extra session one or two times a week in your problem spot.

Measuring Aerobic Endurance: The One-Mile Walking Test

Exercise physiologists often use a tool called the Rockport Walking Test (named after the footwear company) as a way to determine aerobic endurance. The test itself is fairly simple. You'll need a stopwatch (or a watch with a second hand) and some comfortable walking shoes. You can do this test either on the street (you'll need to figure out the distance first with your car odometer) or at a local track. In either case, measure out the exact distance for one mile.

1. Before you begin, take a moment to figure out your heart rate: take your pulse on your neck or wrist for 10 seconds, and then multiply by 6.

   Heart rate before walk: _____ beats per minute

2. Walk the 1-mile distance as fast as you can. Remember to pace yourself; rest or stop along the way if you need to.

3. When you reach the 1-mile mark, stop your watch, and take note of the time. Immediately after this, take your heart rate one more time.

   Time to walk 1 mile: _____ minutes _____ seconds

   Heart rate after walk: _____ beats per minute

4. Take this walking test again at weeks 5 and 9 and at the end of week 12. You should see some progress with both your time and heart rate.

Week 5	Time to walk 1 mile:	_____ minutes _____ seconds
	Heart rate after walk:	_____ beats per minute
Week 9	Time to walk 1 mile:	_____ minutes _____ seconds
	Heart rate after walk:	_____ beats per minute
End of week 12	Time to walk 1 mile:	_____ minutes _____ seconds
	Heart rate after walk:	_____ beats per minute

Simply keeping track of how you feel during and after physical exertion like the one-mile walking test can also give you a good indication of your fitness level. Keep it up, and you'll be certain to see improvements over the course of your training program.

One-Minute Push-Up Test

You can measure both upper-body strength and muscular endurance (how long you can work without fatiguing) by giving yourself a one-minute push-up test. Simply do as many push-ups as you can in one minute. There are a few different ways you can perform this test, depending on your fitness level:

◉ **Beginners:** Stand in front of a sturdy wall with palms on the wall directly under your shoulders; keep your arms straight and back flat. Bend your elbows 90 degrees, bringing your head and upper body toward the wall. Straighten your arms, and return to the starting position. Keep your body in one long line as you press down and push up. Record the number of wall push-ups in 1 minute.

Start of week 1	Wall push-ups in 1 minute: _____
Week 5	Wall push-ups in 1 minute: _____
Week 9	Wall push-ups in 1 minute: _____
End of week 12	Wall push-ups in 1 minute: _____

◉ **Intermediate:** Begin on the floor on all fours, with your palms directly under your shoulders; keep your head and neck aligned with your spine. Bring your knees together, crossing your ankles. Slowly lower your upper body toward the floor, bending your elbows 90 degrees and keeping a straight line from your head to your knees. Straighten your arms to return to start; repeat for 1 minute.

Start of week 1	Knee push-ups in 1 minute: _____
Week 5	Knee push-ups in 1 minute: _____
Week 9	Knee push-ups in 1 minute: _____
End of week 12	Knee push-ups in 1 minute: _____

⊙ **Advanced:** Begin in a full push-up position, with palms on the floor directly under your shoulders and feet about hip distance apart, balancing your body weight on your toes and hands. Lower your upper body toward the floor by bending your elbows 90 degrees and keeping your abs tight, forming a straight line from head to heels. Straighten your arms, and return to start; repeat for 1 minute.

Start of week 1	Full push-ups in 1 minute: _____
Week 5	Full push-ups in 1 minute: _____
Week 9	Full push-ups in 1 minute: _____
End of week 12	Full push-ups in 1 minute: _____

One-Minute Sit-Up Test

The one-minute sit-up test uses the classic sit-up to evaluate abdominal strength and endurance. You'll need a clock or a stopwatch to keep tabs on your time.

Lie on your back with your feet anchored under a sturdy object (such as a couch), or have a partner hold them in place. Clasp your hands behind your head, keeping your elbows pointed out to the sides. Lift your head, neck, shoulders, and back off the floor and sit all the way up, then lower down until the back of your shoulders touch the floor. Continue doing as many sit-ups as possible; keep track of the number of sit-ups you can do (feel free to rest a few seconds if you are unable to sit up continuously). Stop after 1 minute.

Start of week 1	Sit-ups in 1 minute: _____
Week 5	Sit-ups in 1 minute: _____
Week 9	Sit-ups in 1 minute: _____
End of week 12	Sit-ups in 1 minute: _____

One-Minute Chair Squat Test

You can use the one-minute chair squat test to help evaluate the strength and endurance of your lower-body muscles, including your legs and glutes. Using a chair will help you maintain proper form and determine how low you should ideally be going in a squat. You'll need a clock or stopwatch and a standard-size chair.

Stand slightly in front of the chair, with your feet about shoulder distance apart, arms at your sides. Bend your knees and sit back, as if you were going to take a seat in the chair. Your butt should just touch the surface of the seat. Keep your weight in your heels, and don't let your knees shoot past your toes. Stand up and repeat, doing as many squats as you can in 1 minute (feel free to rest a few seconds if you are unable to do the squats continuously).

Start of week 1	Chair squats in 1 minute: _____
Week 5	Chair squats in 1 minute: _____
Week 9	Chair squats in 1 minute: _____
End of week 12	Chair squats in 1 minute: _____

Sit and Reach Test

Another classic fitness test is the sit and reach test, which measures trunk flexion, or how far you can bring your upper body forward while seated. (It's also a good indication of how tight your hamstrings and lower back may be.) To do this test, you'll need a yardstick or tape measure and some tape. Since you should never stretch when cold, warm up for a few minutes by walking or jogging in place. If you can, have a friend or family member measure your results.

Place a yardstick on the floor with the zero mark closest to you; tape it in place at the 15-inch mark. Sit on the floor with the yardstick between your legs and your feet about 12 inches apart. Keep your heels even with the tape at the 15-inch mark. Place one hand over the other so your middle fingers are aligned. Slowly stretch forward, being sure not to bounce or jerk your upper body, and slide your fingertips along the yardstick as far as possible. Do the test 3 times, and then record your best results.

Start of week 1	Sit and reach test (best of 3 tries): _____ in.
Week 5	Sit and reach test (best of 3 tries): _____ in.
Week 9	Sit and reach test (best of 3 tries): _____ in.
End of week 12	Sit and reach test (best of 3 tries): _____ in.

Hamstring Flexibility Test

The hamstring flexibility test, devised by stretching experts Jim and Phil Wharton of Wharton Performance in New York City, is a slightly easier way to estimate your hamstring flexibility (and can also give you a good idea of how flexible the rest of your muscles may be). After warming up for a few minutes, lie on your back with your left knee bent, left foot on the floor, and right leg extended. Loop a rope, sash, or soft belt (like a bathrobe belt) around the ball of your right foot, holding one end in each hand. Lift your right leg as high as you can, pulling gently on the rope. See where you fall in the following range:

Range of Motion	Score
Leg is at 45-degree angle to floor	Tight/poor flexibility
Leg is lifted 90 degrees (perpendicular to body)	Average flexibility
Leg is lifted past 90 degrees (closer to chest)	Very flexible

Retest your flexibility at the different stages of your program.

Start of week 1	Hamstring flexibility: _____
Week 5	Hamstring flexibility: _____
Week 9	Hamstring flexibility: _____
End of week 12	Hamstring flexibility: _____

Upper-Body Flexibility Test

Many of us are notoriously tight in our shoulders and upper back. That's especially true if you sit at a desk for most of the day, rounding forward toward a keyboard, or if you're frequently balancing the phone on one side of your neck and shoulders. To determine your upper-body flexibility, try this "back scratch" arm reach test: Stand up tall with your chest lifted and shoulders pressed down away from your ears. Reach up with your left arm above your head, and then bend your elbow and touch your upper back, between your shoulder blades. Have a friend or family member measure how far you can reach behind your back, noting the distance from the base of your neck to the tip of your middle finger. Repeat the test with the right hand. Next, reach behind your back with your left hand, and try to reach up and touch your right shoulder blade. Measure the distance from the top of your shoulders to the tip of your middle finger. Switch sides and repeat.

TOP ARM REACH

Start of week 1	Left arm: _____	Right arm: _____
Week 5	Left arm: _____	Right arm: _____
Week 9	Left arm: _____	Right arm: _____
End of week 12	Left arm: _____	Right arm: _____

BOTTOM ARM REACH

Start of week 1	Left arm: _____	Right arm: _____
Week 5	Left arm: _____	Right arm: _____
Week 9	Left arm: _____	Right arm: _____
End of week 12	Left arm: _____	Right arm: _____

Standing Balance Drill

Balance is an important part of fitness and of everyday life. A better sense of balance can help you avoid falls (especially important as you get older) and improve your daily function. Balance is also one area in fitness where you are almost certain to notice quick changes in performance.

Stand tall with your feet together in a clear area. Lift your right leg off the floor slightly, raising the foot out to the side or behind you; stay here as long as possible (up to 3 minutes). Record your time, and then repeat with your left leg.

SINGLE-LEG BALANCE

Start of week 1	Right leg: _____	Left leg: _____
Week 5	Right leg: _____	Left leg: _____
Week 9	Right leg: _____	Left leg: _____
End of week 12	Right leg: _____	Left leg: _____

Now try the same exercise with your eyes closed. You'll see how much harder it is to maintain your balance in this position!

EYES-CLOSED BALANCE

Start of week 1	Right leg: _____	Left leg: _____
Week 5	Right leg: _____	Left leg: _____
Week 9	Right leg: _____	Left leg: _____
End of week 12	Right leg: _____	Left leg: _____

WHAT IT ALL MEANS

All of these tests and formulas are meant to give you a good understanding of your current weight, body composition, and fitness levels. Use them to judge where you stand in the program and to help you keep up with your progress along the way. Turn back to this chapter regularly, retest your fitness levels, and record your results. There's nothing more motivating than seeing real progress in black and white!

THE TRICKS
OF THE TRADE

4

N OW THAT YOU HAVE an idea of your fitness starting point (and some guideposts for mapping your progress along the way), it's time to get familiar with some of the equipment and terms that we'll be using in the rest of this book.

WHAT YOU'LL NEED

First off, let's take a look at some of the equipment you'll need for the various exercises presented in the trainer workouts. To a certain extent, you can do the exercises without any equipment at all, using just your body weight for resistance in the strength moves, and using your own two feet for cardio exercises like walking or running. But to challenge your muscles and really see results, at some point you'll need some basic fitness equipment.

When celebrities work with trainers, they often visit the trainers' private workout facilities or have the trainers come to their own well-equipped home gyms. Since many of us don't have the luxury or access to thousand-dollar-plus home equipment or exclusive Hollywood gyms, many of the exercises listed in this book can easily be adapted for home use with some simple, basic workout tools. For those who do have access to a health club or local gym, there are also a variety of machine-based moves that can be used to round out the program.

While you don't have to spend a fortune building a home gym, it does pay to invest in a few key pieces of equipment that will help you keep your muscles challenged and maximize your results. We've given some suggested retail prices for the equipment, most of which is available at sporting goods stores or discounters like Wal-Mart and Target. You can often find used fitness equipment at local garage sales, in classified ads, or even online through websites like eBay and Craigslist. Here are a few of the home gym basics that are called upon in many of the exercises in this book.

Dumbbells

Probably the most popular workout tool for both the home and the gym, dumbbells allow you to target virtually every major muscle group in the body. You'll need a few different weights to work different muscles. Large muscle groups like those in your chest or legs, for example, can handle a significantly greater weight than smaller muscles in your shoulders or arms. While you can purchase individual weights (such as a set of five-pound, ten-pound, and fifteen-pound weights), a better option might be to try a set that allows you to adjust the weights incrementally. These adjustable dumbbells are pricier up front, but you can usually add anywhere from two and a half to five pounds with the turn of a dial. This equipment is definitely a space saver and can even be more affordable than purchasing a complete weight set. If you do choose to purchase only a few individual dumbbells, consider getting a small rack to keep them in place, and buy at least three different sizes so that you're able to keep your muscles challenged.

PRICE: Dumbbells: $1.50–$25.00 each, depending on weight
Adjustable dumbbells: about $250

Exercise Ball

Another basic piece of equipment is one of the large, inflatable exercise balls, which go by several names. Originally used in physical therapy starting in the 1960s, they're often referred to as stability balls, physioballs, and even Swiss balls (because they were initially imported from a Swiss manufacturer). Today you'll find the balls in pretty much any gym or workout facility in the United States. Trainers love them because they're a great way to challenge your core muscles (a.k.a. your abdominal and lower-back muscles), since your body has to constantly engage the core in order to stay balanced on the ball's surface.

Even sitting on the ball can be a challenge. In fact, some trainers recommend their clients replace their standard office chair with a stability ball, so they're working their abs even as they sit at their desk.

While exercise balls are most popular at the gym for ab exercises like crunches, this very versatile piece of equipment can be used for dozens of moves. Some trainers use them in place of a standard weight bench for seated moves like biceps curls and triceps extensions, to work both the abs and the upper body at the same time. They're also a great challenge in lower-body exercises that may require you to balance one or even both legs on the ball's surface.

If you don't have access to a stability ball, you can sometimes substitute a large pillow, such as a sofa cushion, as an alternative when working out at home. It provides some measure of instability, since you'll have to work somewhat harder to stay in form when you are using it instead of a seat or bench.

Stability balls come in different sizes, based on an individual's height. Use the following chart to determine what size to choose. Hint: the more inflated the ball is, the more challenging it will be during the exercise; it's more apt to roll around when it's fully inflated, making it harder to control.

Height	Ball Size
Under 5'0"	45 cm
5'0"–5'8"	55 cm
5'9"–6'3"	65 cm
Over 6'3"	75 cm

PRICE: $15–$25

Resistance Bands/Tubes

Another important type of equipment is stretchable elastic that comes in two main styles: thin rubber tubes (usually with handles attached) and wider bands. The elastic itself provides resistance (thus the name, resistance bands), and they're a great substitute for traditional

Making the most of your home: Weight Substitutions

On a shoestring budget? You can also use some common household items in place of weights. The following chart offers options for turning your pantry into a home gym:

OBJECT	APPROXIMATE WEIGHT
½ liter water bottle or full soup can	1 lb.
1 liter water bottle	2 lb.
½ gallon milk jug	4 lb.
1 gallon milk jug	8 lb.
Backpack or briefcase filled with papers	10–15 lb.

weights because they can be used to work virtually every muscle group, at a fraction of the space and cost. If you attach a band or tube to a stationary object (or simply hold one end or stand on it), you can use it like a weight machine or dumbbell. The nearer to the anchor you hold one end, the more tension you place on the band or tube—and the more challenging the exercise becomes. Bands and tubes come in different levels of resistance. Some are thick enough to challenge even professional athletes.

Many of the trainers in this book give their celebrity clients bands or tubes to use for exercises while they're on location to film a movie or traveling on tour. The resistance devices can easily be thrown into a suitcase or carry-on bag, and using them offers a great way to keep up a current routine when there's no gym or weight room in sight.

In addition to the tubes or bands, you can also buy an inexpensive item called a door anchor that attaches to the tubing and can be easily shut into a door frame. It's a good accessory for upper-body exercises, since it more easily allows you to target the muscles of the chest and back.

PRICE: $5–$10

Medicine Ball

The medicine ball is a classic piece of exercise equipment that dates back to the late 1800s and has been popular with athletes for generations. Trainers love these weighted balls (which generally range in weight from two to fifteen pounds) because using a medicine ball is a good way to target the abdominal muscles, especially the obliques when used in twisting movements. Throwing and catching the ball works the muscles explosively, allowing you to target the different types of muscle fibers and sculpt the abdominals more fully. If you play a sport that involves a twisting or throwing motion (such as golf, tennis, basketball, or volleyball), medicine balls are also a good training tool because they closely mirror the same explosive movements you do to swing a club or racquet or throw a ball. You can throw and catch a ball yourself or find a partner to work with. Some balls also come with handles or ropes for greater variability of exercise.

PRICE: $12 and up

Jump Rope

You don't need to spend a thousand-plus dollars on a treadmill or some other cardiovascular equipment. A jump rope—which can be had for less than $20— is a fantastic way to blast calories while sculpting your arms, shoulders, legs, and butt. It's no wonder boxers and other professional athletes place jumping rope at the center of their conditioning programs.

It might take a little practice, but after just a few sessions, you can take your rope-jumping experience to the next level. Running or skipping in place can keep you going for ten or more minutes, enough to burn almost 150 calories (based on a 145-pound person). If you keep your elbows by your sides, you'll target more of the triceps and get a more efficient rhythm. You'll also improve agility and coordination.

As you get more advanced with jumping rope, vary your workout by incorporating different skips, such as double hops (getting the rope under your feet twice before landing), side-to-side hops, crossovers, high knees, and more. Begin by trying to skip 100 turns without tripping, and progress in increments of 20 to 50.

To sculpt your arms even more and boost your calorie burn, try using a weighted jump rope of one to two pounds.

PRICE: $5–$15

Foam Roller

Another fitness device with roots in physical therapy, large cylindrical foam rollers are favored among trainers as both a stretching device and a core stability aid. Lie on top of the roller to help release sore or overly fatigued muscles and prevent injuries; use it on the floor as an ab-training tool for moves like crunches.

Some trainers in this book say the roller is their favorite new fitness tool because of its simplicity, versatility, and effectiveness.

PRICE: $15

BEEFING UP YOUR FITNESS VOCABULARY

Sometimes a trainer or fitness professional may seem to be speaking a foreign language. But you don't have to be well versed in gymspeak to get the gist of the conversation. You only need to know a few basic terms that the trainers refer to throughout the rest of this book.

● **Strength training:** Anything that places resistance on a muscle to help it get stronger. With strength training, you're actually breaking down the muscle fibers on a microscopic level. The process of the muscle rebuilding itself helps you get stronger and, ultimately, more sculpted. Dumbbells, elastic bands, medicine balls, and even your own body weight can be used to provide this added resistance.

● **Repetitions (reps):** One complete movement of an exercise, including an up-and-down or back-and-forth motion. You'll do several repetitions of each exercise.

● **Sets:** One complete group of repetitions. After you do the suggested number of reps, you'll have finished one set. Most of the exercises here call for two to three sets.

● **Rest:** The amount of time taken between exercises. It's generally a good idea to rest at least one minute between sets of the same exercise, to give your muscles time to recover, so you're able to fully challenge them again in the next set or exercise. In addition to resting between each exercise, you also need to allow your muscles to rest from one workout to the next. Most experts recommend resting a full forty-eight hours before you work the same muscles again. In other words, if you were to do a full total-body workout on a Monday, you should not work any of the muscles again before Wednesday. However, if you were to work only your upper-body muscles on Monday, you could then go ahead and train your lower-body muscles on Tuesday.

● **Resistance:** The amount of weight or effort used to challenge the muscle. You'll read more in the next chapter about how to determine just how much resistance you need to use to get maximum results.

⊙ **Form:** Body position during exercise. It's crucial to maintain proper form throughout your workout, so you maximize results and minimize injury. One good way to do this is to use a mirror while exercising, especially during strength moves. To determine your proper form, follow the form tips given by the trainers and the pictures demonstrating the exercises.

⊙ **Cardiovascular training (cardio; aerobic fitness training):** Essentially any activity that serves to benefit the heart and lungs. Most cardio involves large muscle groups used in a continuous fashion, such as walking, running, cycling, or swimming, and is done for more than just a few minutes.

⊙ **Rate of perceived exertion (RPE):** How hard you are exercising, based on your own exertion levels. In this book, we use RPE on a scale of 1 to 10, with 1 being minimum effort and 10 all-out. In Chapter 12, you'll learn more about using your RPE to determine exactly how hard you should be exercising during a workout. It's especially useful in cardiovascular training, because the more intense the workout, the higher the RPE—and the more calories you'll burn. But go too hard or intense, and you'll either burn out too soon or risk injury. It's important to find the right level of exertion for the exercise.

The celebrity trainers in this book manipulate all of these factors (strength and cardiovascular training, reps, sets, resistance, rest, form, and intensity or RPE) when working with their clients. You'll use all of them as well when you work to reshape your own body. Ready to get started?

5

-LIST
OUT PLANS

KNOW about all the benefits of exercise and what
1 do for you, it's time to get started on your actual
We've put together four different plans, each
it need or goal. Each plan will last twelve weeks.
inner's workout. Use this plan if you're new to exer-
; to exercise after a long layoff, or if your doctor has
:ssary precautions while working out. When you're
:ength moves from Chapters 6 to 11, follow the cues
each move, and avoid exercises that are tagged
"advanced only." Don't worry; you'll get there eventually. But it's important, especially when you're starting out on a fitness program, not to do too much too soon. Otherwise, you might get discouraged or, worse, risk injury. You'll do a mix of strength and low-impact cardio exercises.

The second option is a total-body tone-up. Follow this plan if you want to develop a strong, lean, and sculpted body all over. Depending on your fitness level, you can follow either the beginner or advanced moves. Try the beginner exercises first, and if they seem too easy, then substitute some of the more difficult options. The idea here is to target all of your major muscle groups evenly, while also including some regular cardiovascular training.

The third set of routines is meant to help you target a specific trouble zone. By now, you likely know that you cannot spot-reduce. That means that no matter how hard you try, you'll never lose weight only from a specific body part, like your midsection, thighs, or butt. Instead, by doing regular exercise, including a mix of cardio and strength, you can shed body fat all over. However, while you can't spot-reduce, you can spot-tone: in other words, you can firm up a specific area through targeted exercises designed to build lean muscle mass. If this is your goal, we'll help you focus on busting problem areas like your thighs, butt, arms, and abs through concentrated strength workouts and regular cardio.

Finally, the fourth option focuses on weight loss. While this is not primarily a diet book, losing weight is an important goal for many people. It will take some work on your part, but with an amped-up emphasis on cardio and a full-strength program, safe, healthy weight loss is definitely within reach. For further help in reaching this goal, try following the diet program recommended in Chapter 14.

Even if weight loss is not your primary desire, trainer and nutrition expert Larry Krug offers up many excellent dietary tips that will help you meet your fitness goals. Be sure to turn to Chapter 14 to read all of the ways to include more healthful options in your diet and get more out of every level of this book.

Finally, take a look at the Q-and-A section at the end of this chapter, which addresses the most common concerns and questions regarding the workout programs.

HOW TO PUT THESE PLANS INTO ACTION

Each of the previously mentioned plans is composed of exercises or workouts that appear in our celebrity trainer chapters. We've grouped together different strength moves, along with cardiovascular training, flexibility exercises, and diet tips, to help you reach your better-body goals. Beginners will do a somewhat modified version of strength moves for each muscle group, plus a few days of light cardio and flexibility. Those who wish to tone all over will do several moves for each muscle group and a more intense cardio program, plus the stretching exercises. If you want to target a specific trouble zone (abs, upper body, legs, or butt), you'll do a concentrated group of exercises from each of those areas, along with some more general strength moves to keep your body balanced and, of course, some cardio to burn fat and flexibility to stay healthy. Finally, those with a weight loss goal face a more intensive program that involves several strength moves, more frequent cardio, and consistent flexibility, as well as following the diet suggested in Chapter 14.

A-LIST BEGINNER'S WORKOUT

The best advice we can give a beginner who is starting out is to think like a tortoise, not a hare: start out slow, and don't get discouraged along the way. It takes time to make regular exercise a habit and to see lasting results. Be sure to stick with the entire twelve-week plan, and modify your activity level along the way if you feel at any point the exercises are too much for you.

Elements of the Beginner's Workout

Everyone needs to include all three primary elements of fitness—strength, cardio, and flexibility training—in the workout plan, along with some of the balance training addressed through specific exercises. For beginners, we suggest doing at least one to two exercises from each primary muscle group (Chapters 6 to 11), along with three cardio workouts a week, each lasting from twenty minutes to one hour (Chapter 12). In addition, you should include the flexibility exercises in Chapter 13 at least three days a week (more if you can fit them in). On off days, try to do some small amount of activity, even if it's just walking for ten to twenty minutes around the neighborhood or on a treadmill. For the strength moves, a good beginner option is to use resistance bands where indicated instead of weights.

Sample Beginner's Workout Plan

If you're a beginner, follow the suggested routines on pages 46–48. If you don't have access to the given equipment, you can switch around the exercises with other moves for each muscle group.

BEGINNER'S WORKOUT PLAN

WEEKS 1–4

MONDAY: STRENGTH

Do 1 to 2 sets, 13 to 15 reps per set, of each of the following exercises:

▶ Band series (page 84; works arms, chest)
▶ Standing cross-country skiing with band (page 97; works shoulders)
▶ Seated one-arm pull (page 104; works shoulders)
▶ Lat extension (page 114; works back)
▶ Back extension on ball (page 118; works back)
▶ Ball squat (page 139; works legs, butt)
▶ Hip bridge (page 140; works legs, butt)
▶ Side lunge (page 155; works legs, butt)
▶ Bent-knee hundred (page 124; works abs)
▶ Three-part crunch combo (page 129; works abs)
ESTIMATED CALORIES BURNED: 100*

TUESDAY: CARDIO AND FLEXIBILITY

➲ **Cardio:** Aerobic base training. Walk for 20 to 30 minutes at moderate intensity, or do any other low-impact aerobic activity, such as swimming, cycling, or elliptical machine, for 20 to 30 minutes. (For details, see page 168.)
➲ **Flexibility:** Do all of the stretches shown in Chapter 13 (page 186).
ESTIMATED CALORIES BURNED: 260–375

WEDNESDAY: OFF

Optional: Walk for 20 minutes.
ESTIMATED CALORIES BURNED: 0–150

THURSDAY: STRENGTH

Repeat Monday's exercises.
ESTIMATED CALORIES BURNED: 100

FRIDAY: CARDIO AND FLEXIBILITY

➲ **Cardio:** Aerobic base training. Walk for 20 to 30 minutes at moderate intensity, or do any other low-impact aerobic activity, such as swimming, cycling, or elliptical machine, for 20 to 30 minutes.
➲ **Flexibility:** Do all of the stretches shown in Chapter 13 (page 186).
ESTIMATED CALORIES BURNED: 260–375

SATURDAY: OFF

Optional: Walk for 20 minutes.
ESTIMATED CALORIES BURNED: 0–150

SUNDAY: CARDIO AND FLEXIBILITY

➲ **Cardio:** Aerobic base training. Walk for 20 to 30 minutes at moderate intensity, or do any other low-impact aerobic activity, such as swimming, cycling, or elliptical machine, for 20 to 30 minutes.
➲ **Flexibility:** Do all of the stretches shown in Chapter 13 (page 186).
ESTIMATED CALORIES BURNED: 260–375

*All calories based on a 150-pound person.

TOTAL WEEKLY CALORIES BURNED: 980–1,625

MONDAY: STRENGTH

Do 1 to 2 sets, 10 to 12 reps per set, of each of the following exercises:

- Stability ball incline plank (page 83; works arms, chest)
- Bridge chest press (page 89; works arms, chest)
- Overhead press (page 117; works back and shoulders)
- One-arm dumbbell row plus lunge (page 112; works back, legs, butt)
- Dumbbell upright row (page 100; works shoulders)
- Reverse lunge (page 143; works legs, butt)
- Lateral lunge (page 142; works legs, butt)
- Reverse hyperextension on ball (page 157; works abs, back, butt)
- Roll-up with ball (page 126; works abs)
- Plank pull (page 131; works abs)

ESTIMATED CALORIES BURNED: 125

TUESDAY: CARDIO AND FLEXIBILITY

➲ **Cardio:** Aerobic base training. Walk for 25 to 35 minutes at moderate intensity, or do any other low-impact aerobic activity, such as swimming, cycling, or elliptical machine, for 25 to 35 minutes.

➲ **Flexibility:** Do all of the stretches shown in Chapter 13 (page 186).

ESTIMATED CALORIES BURNED: 250–440

WEDNESDAY: OFF

Optional: Walk for 30 minutes.

ESTIMATED CALORIES BURNED: 225

THURSDAY: STRENGTH

Repeat Monday's exercises.

ESTIMATED CALORIES BURNED: 125

FRIDAY: CARDIO/INTERVAL TRAINING

After building up your aerobic base for one month, it's time to increase the challenge by adding an interval workout to your mix. By incorporating periodic bursts of intensity, followed by a more moderate recovery period, you'll burn at least 50 percent more calories than doing a moderate workout for the same amount of time. (See page 170 for more information on the benefits of interval training.)

Do the 35-minute interval routine for beginners (page 171).

ESTIMATED CALORIES BURNED: 350–450

SATURDAY: OFF

Optional: Walk for 30 minutes.

ESTIMATED CALORIES BURNED: 225

SUNDAY: CARDIO AND FLEXIBILITY

➲ **Cardio:** Aerobic base training. Walk for 25 to 35 minutes at moderate intensity, or do any other low-impact aerobic activity for 25 to 35 minutes.

➲ **Flexibility:** Do all of the stretches shown in Chapter 13 (page 186).

ESTIMATED CALORIES BURNED: 250–440

TOTAL WEEKLY CALORIES BURNED: 1,550–2,030

MONDAY: STRENGTH

Do 1 to 2 sets, 8 to 10 reps per set, of each of the following exercises:

- Diamond push-up on knees, no ball (page 82; works arms, chest)
- Overhead triceps extension on ball (page 90; works arms)
- Anterior and lateral dumbbell T-raise (page 101; works shoulders)
- High band row (page 115; works back)
- Split squat (page 141; works legs, butt)
- Romanian dead lift (page 144; works legs, butt)
- Staggered squat (page 156; works legs, butt)
- Butt blaster (page 159; works butt)
- Tuck slide (page 125; works abs)
- Around the world (page 127; works abs)

ESTIMATED CALORIES BURNED: 125

TUESDAY: CARDIO AND FLEXIBILITY

⊙ **Cardio:** Aerobic base training. Walk for 30 to 45 minutes at moderate intensity, or do any other low-impact aerobic activity, such as swimming, cycling, or elliptical machine, for 30 to 45 minutes (for details, see page 168).

⊙ **Flexibility:** Do all of the stretches shown in Chapter 13 (page 186).

ESTIMATED CALORIES BURNED: 300–560

WEDNESDAY: OFF

Optional: Walk for 30 minutes.

ESTIMATED CALORIES BURNED: 225

THURSDAY: STRENGTH

Repeat Monday's exercises.

ESTIMATED CALORIES BURNED: 125

FRIDAY: CARDIO

⊙ **Interval training:** Do the 35-minute interval routine for beginners (page 171).

ESTIMATED CALORIES BURNED: 350–450

SATURDAY: OFF

Optional: Walk for 30 minutes.

ESTIMATED CALORIES BURNED: 225

SUNDAY: CARDIO AND FLEXIBILITY

⊙ **Cardio:** Aerobic base training. Walk for 30 to 45 minutes at moderate intensity, or do any other low-impact aerobic activity for 30 to 45 minutes.

⊙ **Flexibility:** Do all of the stretches shown in Chapter 13 (page 186).

ESTIMATED CALORIES BURNED: 300–560

TOTAL WEEKLY CALORIES BURNED: 1,200–1,710

TOTAL BODY TONE-UP

If you're looking to get strong and sculpted everywhere and don't have a primary weight loss goal, this is the plan for you. You'll still be doing a combination of cardio and strength moves, but at a slightly higher intensity and frequency than in the beginner plan. Start by trying some of the beginner modifications, and then move up to the advanced moves toward the end of the plan (or just adapt what seems right for your own fitness level). After a few weeks, you'll notice a change in your strength, endurance, and appearance. Take the tests in Chapter 3 after the first four weeks, then again after eight weeks, to check on your body composition, weight, body fat, and other measurements, along with your strength, cardio, and flexibility gains.

Elements of the Total Body Tone-Up Routine

You'll be doing a mix of strength, cardio, and flexibility, with some balance drills thrown into the strength moves. For the strength workouts, you'll do two to three exercises for each primary muscle group twice a week (Chapters 6 to 11), using a weight that's heavy enough to fatigue the muscles by the final rep. You'll also do three days of cardio activity and one circuit routine that combines cardio and strength. If this six-day-a-week plan is too much to fit into your schedule, do one extra circuit workout on your strength day, or do your cardio and strength back to back on the same day. As in the beginner's plan, if you have time on your off day, try to include some small amount of activity, even if it's just a brief walk around the neighborhood or on a treadmill.

TOTAL BODY TONE-UP ROUTINE

WEEKS 1–4

MONDAY: STRENGTH

Do 2 to 3 sets, 13 to 15 reps per set, of each of the following exercises:

▶ Band series (page 84; works arms, chest)
▶ Stability ball incline plank (page 83; works arms, chest)
▶ Back extension on ball (page 118; works back)
▶ One-arm cable row with rotation (page 113; works back)
▶ Anterior and lateral dumbbell T-raise (page 101; works shoulders)
▶ Rear delt dumbbell fly (page 102; works shoulders)
▶ Reaching lunge (page 153; works legs, butt)
▶ Butt blaster (page 159; works butt)
▶ Ball squat (page 139; works legs, butt)
▶ Rotational step-up (page 146; works legs, butt)
▶ Bent-knee hundred (page 124; works abs)
▶ Plank pull (page 131; works abs)

ESTIMATED CALORIES BURNED: 270*

TUESDAY: CARDIO AND FLEXIBILITY

➲ Cardio—steady-state workout: Choose any cardio activity—walking, running, swimming, cycling, etc.—that you can sustain at a moderately high intensity for 45 to 50 minutes (for details, see page 170).
➲ Flexibility: Do all of the stretches shown in Chapter 13 (page 186).

ESTIMATED CALORIES BURNED: 500–775

WEDNESDAY: STRENGTH

Repeat Monday's workout.
ESTIMATED CALORIES BURNED: 270

THURSDAY: CARDIO

Interval workout, 35 minutes: Follow the interval program on page 171 to blast more calories and fat while improving your aerobic fitness.
ESTIMATED CALORIES BURNED: 500–600

FRIDAY: OFF

SATURDAY: CARDIO/STRENGTH CIRCUIT

Follow either the no-weight or weight option circuits on pages 172–181 to burn fat while sculpting all your major muscle groups.
ESTIMATED CALORIES BURNED: 325–450

SUNDAY: CARDIO AND FLEXIBILITY

➲ Cardio—steady-state workout: Choose any cardio activity—walking, running, swimming, cycling, etc.—that you can sustain at a moderately high intensity for 45 to 50 minutes (for details, see page 170).
➲ Flexibility: Do all of the stretches shown in Chapter 13 (page 186).

ESTIMATED CALORIES BURNED: 500–775

*All calories based on a 150-pound person.

TOTAL WEEKLY CALORIES BURNED: 2,365–3,140

MONDAY: STRENGTH

Do 2 to 3 sets, 10 to 12 reps per set, of each of the following exercises:

▶ Diamond push-up with medicine ball (page 82; works arms, chest)
▶ Bridge chest press (page 89; works arms, chest)
▶ One-arm dumbbell row plus lunge (page 112; works back, legs, butt)
▶ Overhead press (page 117; works back, shoulders)
▶ Anterior pull (page 96; works shoulders)
▶ Seated one-arm pull (page 104; works back, shoulders)
▶ Twisting lunge (page 154; works legs, butt)
▶ Staggered squat (page 156; works legs, butt)
▶ Hip bridge (page 140; works butt)
▶ Romanian dead lift (page 144; works legs, butt)
▶ Tuck slide (page 125; works abs)
▶ Roll-up with ball (page 126; works abs)

ESTIMATED CALORIES BURNED: 270

TUESDAY: CARDIO AND FLEXIBILITY

◐ Cardio—steady-state workout: Choose any cardio activity—walking, running, swimming, cycling, etc.—that you can sustain at a moderately high intensity for 45 to 50 minutes (for details, see page 170).

◐ Flexibility: Do all of the stretches shown in Chapter 13 (page 186).

ESTIMATED CALORIES BURNED: 550–825

WEDNESDAY: STRENGTH

Repeat Monday's workout.

ESTIMATED CALORIES BURNED: 270

THURSDAY: CARDIO

Interval workout, 35 minutes: Follow the interval program on page 171 to blast more calories and fat while improving your aerobic fitness.

ESTIMATED CALORIES BURNED: 500–600

FRIDAY: OFF

SATURDAY: CARDIO/STRENGTH CIRCUIT

Follow either the no-weight or weight option circuits on pages 172–181 to burn fat while sculpting all your major muscle groups.

ESTIMATED CALORIES BURNED: 325–450

SUNDAY: CARDIO/FLEXIBILITY

◐ Cardio—steady-state workout: Choose any cardio activity—walking, running, swimming, cycling, etc.—that you can sustain at a moderately high intensity for 45 to 50 minutes (for details, see page 170).

◐ Flexibility: Do all of the stretches shown in Chapter 13 (page 186).

ESTIMATED CALORIES BURNED: 550–825

TOTAL WEEKLY CALORIES BURNED: 2,465–3,240

MONDAY: STRENGTH

Do 2 to 3 sets, 8 to 10 reps per set, of each of the following exercises:

- ▶ Horizontal pull-up (page 81; works arms, chest)
- ▶ Overhead press on ball (page 117; works arms)
- ▶ Lat extension (page 114; works back)
- ▶ High band row (page 115; works abs, back)
- ▶ Standing cross-country skiing with band (page 97; works shoulders)
- ▶ One-arm cross-band lateral (page 98; works shoulders)
- ▶ Side lunge (page 155; works legs, butt)
- ▶ Single-leg hip bridge (page 158; works butt)
- ▶ Split squat (page 141; works legs, butt)
- ▶ Calf raise (page 147; works legs)
- ▶ Around the world (page 127; works abs)
- ▶ Three-part crunch combo (page 129; works abs)

ESTIMATED CALORIES BURNED: 270

TUESDAY: CARDIO AND FLEXIBILITY

↻ **Cardio—steady-state workout:** Choose any cardio activity—walking, running, swimming, cycling, etc.—that you can sustain at a moderately high intensity for 50 to 60 minutes (for details, see page 170).

↻ **Flexibility:** Do all of the stretches shown in Chapter 13 (page 186).

ESTIMATED CALORIES BURNED: 475–900

WEDNESDAY: STRENGTH

Repeat Monday's workout.

ESTIMATED CALORIES BURNED: 270

THURSDAY: CARDIO

Interval workout, 35 minutes: Follow the interval program on page 171 to blast more calories and fat while improving your aerobic fitness.

ESTIMATED CALORIES BURNED: 500–600

FRIDAY: OFF

SATURDAY: CARDIO/STRENGTH CIRCUIT

Follow either the no-weight or weight option circuits on pages 172–181 to burn fat while sculpting all your major muscle groups.

ESTIMATED CALORIES BURNED: 325–450

SUNDAY: CARDIO/FLEXIBILITY

↻ **Cardio—steady-state workout:** Choose any cardio activity—walking, running, swimming, cycling, etc.—that you can sustain at a moderately high intensity for 50 to 60 minutes (for details, see page 170).

↻ **Flexibility:** Do all of the stretches shown in Chapter 13 (page 186).

ESTIMATED CALORIES BURNED: 475–900

TOTAL WEEKLY CALORIES BURNED: 2,315–3,390

TARGET YOUR TROUBLE ZONES

Is a flabby middle your main concern? Or would you rather say sayonara to saddlebags? Maybe you've got a bottom that needs boosting, or jiggly arms that could use firming. If you've got a specific trouble zone you'd like to attack, this is the place to start.

As we've already discussed, it's impossible to get rid of fat in just one area of your body. But exercising with a combination of aerobic activity to lose fat everywhere plus building muscle with specific moves will put you well on your way to terminating your body's biggest trouble zones.

Elements of the Trouble Zone Workouts

You'll still need to do a combo of cardio workouts to burn fat everywhere plus a variety of strength moves to build lean muscle in your target area (and a few other exercises to keep your muscles in balance). And, of course, don't forget to do some flexibility training to increase your range of motion and help you avoid injury. This plan includes three days of strength and four days of cardio (you'll need to do both of them back to back a couple of times each week), plus one circuit routine that combines cardio and strength into one session. If you find it difficult to fit all this into your schedule, add one extra circuit routine in place of a cardio/strength day.

We've got three different trouble zone tamers for you to choose from: one for a sleek upper body, one for lean legs and butt, and the third for flat, sexy abs. The principles for each are the same: you'll do at least three to four exercises for your specific trouble zone, along with two to three additional moves to keep the rest of your body in balance (many of which also peripherally work the target muscles). Follow the same cardio and flexibility programs for all three workouts.

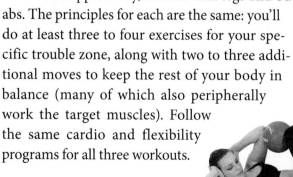

TARGET: SCULPTED ARMS AND SHOULDERS

WEEKS 1–4

MONDAY: STRENGTH

Do 2 to 3 sets, 13 to 15 reps per set, of each of the following exercises:

- Band series (page 84; works arms, chest)
- Stability ball incline plank (page 83; works arms, chest)
- Horizontal pull-up (page 81; works arms, chest)
- One-arm cable row with rotation (page 113; works back, abs, arms)
- Anterior and lateral dumbbell T-raise (page 101; works shoulders)
- Rear delt dumbbell fly (page 102; works shoulders)
- Reaching lunge (page 153; works legs, butt)
- Rotational step-up (page 146; works legs, butt)
- Three-part crunch combo (page 129; works abs)

ESTIMATED CALORIES BURNED: 225*

TUESDAY: CARDIO AND FLEXIBILITY

⊙ Cardio—interval workout, 35 minutes: Follow the interval program on page 171 to blast more calories and fat while improving your aerobic fitness.

⊙ Flexibility: Do all of the stretches shown in Chapter 13 (page 186).

ESTIMATED CALORIES BURNED: 575–675

WEDNESDAY: STRENGTH AND CARDIO

⊙ Strength: Repeat Monday's workout.

⊙ Cardio—steady-state workout: Choose any cardio activity—walking, running, cycling, etc.—that you can sustain at a moderately high intensity for 30 to 45 minutes (for details, see page 170).

ESTIMATED CALORIES BURNED: 550–965

THURSDAY: CARDIO/STRENGTH CIRCUIT

Follow either the no-weight or weight option circuits on pages 172–181 to burn fat while sculpting all your major muscle groups.

ESTIMATED CALORIES BURNED: 325–450

FRIDAY: OFF

SATURDAY: STRENGTH AND FLEXIBILITY

⊙ Strength: Repeat Monday's workout.

⊙ Flexibility: Repeat Tuesday's flexibility workout.

ESTIMATED CALORIES BURNED: 300

SUNDAY: CARDIO

⊙ Steady-state workout: Choose any cardio activity—walking, running, cycling, etc.—that you can sustain at a moderately high intensity for 45 to 50 minutes (for details, see page 170).

ESTIMATED CALORIES BURNED: 340–750

*All calories based on a 150-pound person.

TOTAL WEEKLY CALORIES BURNED: 2,315–3,365

MONDAY: STRENGTH

Do 2 to 3 sets, 10 to 12 reps per set, of each of the following exercises:

▶ Diamond push-up with medicine ball (page 82; works arms, chest)
▶ Bridge chest press (page 89; works arms, chest)
▶ One-arm dumbbell row plus lunge (page 112; works back, legs, butt)
▶ Overhead press (page 117; works back, shoulders)
▶ Anterior and lateral dumbbell T-raise (page 101; works shoulders)
▶ Back extension on ball (page 118; works back)
▶ Seated one-arm pull (page 104; works shoulders)
▶ Twisting lunge (page 154; works legs, butt)
▶ Staggered squat (page 156; works legs, butt)
▶ Tuck slide (page 125; works abs)

ESTIMATED CALORIES BURNED: 225

TUESDAY: CARDIO AND FLEXIBILITY

⊘ **Cardio—interval workout, 35 minutes:** Follow the interval program on page 171 to blast more calories and fat while improving your aerobic fitness.

⊘ **Flexibility:** Do all of the stretches shown in Chapter 13 (page 186).

ESTIMATED CALORIES BURNED: 575–675

WEDNESDAY: STRENGTH AND CARDIO

⊘ **Strength:** Repeat Monday's workout.

⊘ **Cardio—steady-state workout:** Choose any cardio activity—walking, running, swimming, cycling, etc.—that you can sustain at a moderately high intensity for 40 to 50 minutes (for details, see page 170).

ESTIMATED CALORIES BURNED: 540–1,025

THURSDAY: CARDIO/STRENGTH CIRCUIT

Follow either the no-weight or weight option circuits on pages 172–181 to burn fat while sculpting all your major muscle groups.

ESTIMATED CALORIES BURNED: 325–450

FRIDAY: OFF

SATURDAY: STRENGTH AND FLEXIBILITY

⊘ **Strength:** Repeat Monday's workout.
⊘ **Flexibility:** Repeat Tuesday's flexibility workout.

ESTIMATED CALORIES BURNED: 300

SUNDAY: CARDIO

⊘ **Steady-state workout:** Choose any cardio activity—walking, running, swimming, cycling, etc.—that you can sustain at a moderately high intensity for 45 to 60 minutes (for details, see page 170).

ESTIMATED CALORIES BURNED: 350–800

TOTAL WEEKLY CALORIES BURNED: 2,315–3,475

MONDAY: STRENGTH

Do 2 to 3 sets, 8 to 10 reps per set, of each of the following exercises:

▶ Medicine ball partner toss (page 88; works arms, chest)
▶ Overhead triceps extension on ball (page 90; works arms)
▶ Lat extension (page 114; works back)
▶ High band row (page 115; works back, abs)
▶ Dumbbell upright row (page 100; works back, shoulders)
▶ Standing cross-country skiing with band (page 97; works shoulders)
▶ One-arm cross-band lateral (page 98; works shoulders)
▶ Side lunge (page 155; works legs, butt)
▶ Split squat (page 141; works legs, butt)
▶ Around the world (page 127; works abs)

ESTIMATED CALORIES BURNED: 225

TUESDAY: CARDIO AND FLEXIBILITY

⊙ **Cardio—interval workout, 35 minutes:** Follow the interval program on page 171 to blast more calories and fat while improving your aerobic fitness.
⊙ **Flexibility:** Do all of the stretches shown in Chapter 13 (page 186).

ESTIMATED CALORIES BURNED: 575–675

WEDNESDAY: STRENGTH AND CARDIO

⊙ **Strength:** Repeat Monday's workout.

⊙ **Cardio—steady-state workout:** Choose any cardio activity—walking, running, swimming, cycling, etc.—that you can sustain at a moderately high intensity for 45 to 55 minutes (for details, see page 170).

ESTIMATED CALORIES BURNED: 565–1,050

THURSDAY: CARDIO/STRENGTH CIRCUIT

Follow either the no-weight or weight option circuits on pages 172–181 to burn fat while sculpting all your major muscle groups.

ESTIMATED CALORIES BURNED: 325–450

FRIDAY: OFF

SATURDAY: STRENGTH AND FLEXIBILITY

⊙ **Strength:** Repeat Monday's workout.
⊙ **Flexibility:** Repeat Tuesday's flexibility workout.

ESTIMATED CALORIES BURNED: 300

SUNDAY: CARDIO

⊙ **Steady-state workout:** Choose any cardio activity—walking, running, swimming, cycling, etc.—that you can sustain at a moderately high intensity for 50 to 60 minutes (for details, see page 170).

ESTIMATED CALORIES BURNED: 375–900

TOTAL WEEKLY CALORIES BURNED: 2,365–3,600

TARGET: SLEEK THIGHS, FIRM BUTT

MONDAY: STRENGTH

Do 2 to 3 sets, 13 to 15 reps per set, of each of the following exercises:

- Reaching lunge (page 153; works legs, butt)
- Butt blaster (page 159; works legs, butt)
- Ball squat (page 139; works legs, butt)
- Rotational step-up (page 146; works legs, butt)
- Calf raise (page 147; works legs)
- Band series (page 84; works arms, chest)
- Bent-knee hundred (page 124; works abs)

ESTIMATED CALORIES BURNED: 225*

TUESDAY: CARDIO AND FLEXIBILITY

➲ **Cardio—interval workout, 35 minutes:** Follow the interval program on page 171 to blast more calories and fat while improving your aerobic fitness.

➲ **Flexibility:** Do all of the stretches shown in Chapter 13 (page 186).

ESTIMATED CALORIES BURNED: 575–675

WEDNESDAY: STRENGTH AND CARDIO

➲ **Strength:** Repeat Monday's workout.

➲ **Cardio—steady-state workout:** Choose any cardio activity (walking, running, swimming, cycling, etc.) that you can sustain at a moderately high intensity for 30 to 45 minutes (for details, see page 170).

ESTIMATED CALORIES BURNED: 550–965

THURSDAY: CARDIO/STRENGTH CIRCUIT

Follow either the no-weight or weight option circuits on pages 172–181 to burn fat while sculpting all your major muscle groups.

ESTIMATED CALORIES BURNED: 325–450

FRIDAY: OFF

SATURDAY: STRENGTH AND FLEXIBILITY

➲ **Strength:** Repeat Monday's workout.
➲ **Flexibility:** Repeat Tuesday's flexibility workout.

ESTIMATED CALORIES BURNED: 300

SUNDAY: CARDIO

➲ **Steady-state workout:** Choose any cardio activity (walking, running, swimming, cycling, etc.) that you can sustain at a moderately high intensity for 45 to 50 minutes (for details, see page 170).

ESTIMATED CALORIES BURNED: 340–750

*All calories based on a 150-pound person.

TOTAL WEEKLY CALORIES BURNED: 2,315–3,365

MONDAY: STRENGTH

Do 2 to 3 sets, 10 to 12 reps per set, of each of the following exercises:

- Twisting lunge (page 154; works legs, butt)
- Staggered squat (page 156; works legs, butt)
- Hip bridge (page 140; works butt)
- Romanian dead lift (page 144; works legs, butt)
- Calf raise (page 147; works legs)
- Stability ball incline plank (page 83; works arms, chest)
- Anterior and lateral dumbbell T-raise (page 101; works shoulders)
- Tuck slide (page 125; works abs)

ESTIMATED CALORIES BURNED: 225

TUESDAY: CARDIO AND FLEXIBILITY

⊙ **Cardio—interval workout, 35 minutes:** Follow the interval program on page 171 to blast more calories and fat while improving your aerobic fitness.

⊙ **Flexibility:** Do all of the stretches shown in Chapter 13 (page 186).

ESTIMATED CALORIES BURNED: 575–675

WEDNESDAY: STRENGTH AND CARDIO

⊙ **Strength:** Repeat Monday's workout.

⊙ **Cardio—steady-state workout:** Choose any cardio activity—walking, running, swimming, cycling, etc.—that you can sustain at a moderately high intensity for 40 to 50 minutes (for details, see page 170).

ESTIMATED CALORIES BURNED: 540–1,025

THURSDAY: CARDIO/STRENGTH CIRCUIT

Follow either the no-weight or weight option circuits on pages 172–181 to burn fat while sculpting all your major muscle groups.

ESTIMATED CALORIES BURNED: 325–450

FRIDAY: OFF

SATURDAY: STRENGTH AND FLEXIBILITY

⊙ **Strength:** Repeat Monday's workout.

⊙ **Flexibility:** Repeat Tuesday's flexibility workout.

ESTIMATED CALORIES BURNED: 300

SUNDAY: CARDIO

⊙ **Steady-state workout:** Choose any cardio activity—walking, running, swimming, cycling, etc.—that you can sustain at a moderately high intensity for 45 to 60 minutes (for details, see page 170).

ESTIMATED CALORIES BURNED: 350–800

TOTAL WEEKLY CALORIES BURNED: 2,315–3,475

MONDAY: STRENGTH

Do 2 to 3 sets, 8 to 10 reps per set, of each of the following exercises:

▶ Side lunge (page 155; works legs, butt)
▶ Single-leg hip bridge (page 158; works legs, butt)
▶ Split squat (page 141; works legs, butt)
▶ Reverse lunge (page 143; works legs, butt)
▶ Calf raise (page 147; works legs)
▶ Diamond push-up with ball (page 82; works arms, chest)
▶ One-arm dumbbell row plus lunge (page 112; works back, legs, butt)
▶ Three-part crunch combo (page 129; works abs)

ESTIMATED CALORIES BURNED: 225

TUESDAY: CARDIO AND FLEXIBILITY

⊙ **Cardio—interval workout, 35 minutes:** Follow the interval program on page 141 to blast more calories and fat while improving your aerobic fitness.
⊙ **Flexibility:** Do all of the stretches shown in Chapter 13 (page 186).

ESTIMATED CALORIES BURNED: 575–675

WEDNESDAY: STRENGTH AND CARDIO

⊙ **Strength:** Repeat Monday's workout.
⊙ **Cardio—steady-state workout:** Choose any cardio activity—walking, running, swimming, cycling, etc.—that you can sustain at a moderately high intensity for 45 to 55 minutes (for details, see page 170).

ESTIMATED CALORIES BURNED: 565–1,050

THURSDAY: CARDIO/STRENGTH CIRCUIT

Follow either the no-weight or weight-option circuits on pages 172–181 to burn fat while sculpting all your major muscle groups.

ESTIMATED CALORIES BURNED: 325–450

FRIDAY: OFF

SATURDAY: STRENGTH AND FLEXIBILITY

⊙ **Strength:** Repeat Monday's workout.
⊙ **Flexibility:** Repeat Tuesday's flexibility workout.

ESTIMATED CALORIES BURNED: 300

SUNDAY: CARDIO

⊙ **Steady-state workout:** Choose any cardio activity—walking, running, swimming, cycling, etc.—that you can sustain at a moderately high intensity for 50 to 60 minutes (for details, see page 170).

ESTIMATED CALORIES BURNED: 375–900

TOTAL WEEKLY CALORIES BURNED: 2,365–3,600

TARGET: FLAT, SEXY ABS

WEEKS 1–4

MONDAY: STRENGTH

Do 2 to 3 sets, 13 to 15 reps per set, of each of the following exercises:

- Bent-knee hundred (page 124; works abs)
- Tuck slide (page 125; works abs)
- Roll-up with ball (page 126; works abs)
- Diamond push-up with medicine ball (page 82; works abs, arms, chest)
- One-arm cable row with rotation (page 113; works back, abs)
- Reverse hyperextension on ball (page 157; works abs, butt)
- Split squat (page 141; works legs, butt)

ESTIMATED CALORIES BURNED: 225*

TUESDAY: CARDIO AND FLEXIBILITY

→ **Cardio—interval workout, 35 minutes:** Follow the interval program on page 171 to blast more calories and fat while improving your aerobic fitness.

→ **Flexibility:** Do all of the stretches shown in Chapter 13 (page 186).

ESTIMATED CALORIES BURNED: 575–675

WEDNESDAY: STRENGTH AND CARDIO

→ **Strength:** Repeat Monday's workout.

→ **Cardio—steady-state workout:** Choose any cardio activity—walking, running, swimming, cycling, etc.—that you can sustain at a moderately high intensity for 30 to 45 minutes (for details, see page 170).

ESTIMATED CALORIES BURNED: 550–965

THURSDAY: CARDIO/STRENGTH CIRCUIT

Follow either the no-weight or weight option circuits on pages 172–181 to burn fat while sculpting all your major muscle groups.

ESTIMATED CALORIES BURNED: 325–450

FRIDAY: OFF

SATURDAY: STRENGTH AND FLEXIBILITY

→ **Strength:** Repeat Monday's workout.

→ **Flexibility:** Repeat Tuesday's flexibility workout.

ESTIMATED CALORIES BURNED: 300

SUNDAY: CARDIO

→ **Steady-state workout:** Choose any cardio activity—walking, running, swimming, cycling, etc.—that you can sustain at a moderately high intensity for 45 to 50 minutes (for details, see page 170).

ESTIMATED CALORIES BURNED: 340–750

*All calories based on a 150-pound person.

TOTAL WEEKLY CALORIES BURNED: 2,315–3,475

MONDAY: STRENGTH

Do 2 to 3 sets, 10 to 12 reps per set, of each of the following exercises:

▶ Bent-knee hundred (page 124; works abs)
▶ Plank pull (page 131; works abs)
▶ Three-part crunch combo (page 129; works abs)
▶ Stability ball incline plank (page 83; works abs, arms, chest)
▶ One-arm cross-band lateral (page 98; works shoulders)
▶ Ball squat (page 139; works legs, butt)
▶ Hip bridge (page 140; works butt)

ESTIMATED CALORIES BURNED: 225

TUESDAY: CARDIO AND FLEXIBILITY

◎ **Cardio—interval workout, 35 minutes:** Follow the interval program on page 171 to blast more calories and fat while improving your aerobic fitness.
◎ **Flexibility:** Do all of the stretches shown in Chapter 13 (page 186).

ESTIMATED CALORIES BURNED: 575–675

WEDNESDAY: STRENGTH AND CARDIO

◎ **Strength:** Repeat Monday's workout.
◎ **Cardio—steady-state workout:** Choose any cardio activity—walking, running, swimming, cycling, etc.—that you can sustain at a moderately high intensity for 40 to 50 minutes (for details, see page 170).

ESTIMATED CALORIES BURNED: 540–1,025

THURSDAY: CARDIO/STRENGTH CIRCUIT

Follow either the no-weight or weight option circuits on pages 172–181 to burn fat while sculpting all your major muscle groups.

ESTIMATED CALORIES BURNED: 325–450

FRIDAY: OFF

SATURDAY: STRENGTH AND FLEXIBILITY

◎ **Strength:** Repeat Monday's workout.
◎ **Flexibility:** Repeat Tuesday's flexibility workout.

ESTIMATED CALORIES BURNED: 300

SUNDAY: CARDIO

◎ **Steady-state workout:** Choose any cardio activity—walking, running, swimming, cycling, etc.—that you can sustain at a moderately high intensity for 45 to 60 minutes (for details, see page 170).

ESTIMATED CALORIES BURNED: 350–800

TOTAL WEEKLY CALORIES BURNED: 2,315–3,475

MONDAY: STRENGTH

Do 2 to 3 sets, 8 to 10 reps per set, of each of the following exercises:

- ▶ Bent-knee hundred (page 124; works abs)
- ▶ Around the world (page 127; works abs)
- ▶ Tuck slide (page 125; works abs)
- ▶ Roll-up with ball (page 126; works abs)
- ▶ Medicine ball partner toss (page 88; works abs, arms, chest)
- ▶ Reverse hyperextension on ball (page 157; works abs, back)
- ▶ Twisting lunge (page 154; works legs, butt)
- ▶ Rotational step-up (page 146; works legs, butt)

ESTIMATED CALORIES BURNED: 225

TUESDAY: CARDIO AND FLEXIBILITY

⊃ **Cardio—interval workout, 35 minutes:** Follow the interval program on page 171 to blast more calories and fat while improving your aerobic fitness.

⊃ **Flexibility:** Do all of the stretches shown in Chapter 13 (page 186).

ESTIMATED CALORIES BURNED: 575–675

WEDNESDAY: STRENGTH AND CARDIO

⊃ **Strength:** Repeat Monday's workout.

⊃ **Cardio—steady-state workout:** Choose any cardio activity—walking, running, swimming, cycling, etc.—that you can sustain at a moderately high intensity for 45 to 55 minutes (for details, see page 170).

ESTIMATED CALORIES BURNED: 565–1,050

THURSDAY: CARDIO/STRENGTH CIRCUIT

Follow either the no-weight or weight option circuits on pages 172–181 to burn fat while sculpting all your major muscle groups.

ESTIMATED CALORIES BURNED: 325–450

FRIDAY: OFF

SATURDAY: STRENGTH AND FLEXIBILITY

⊃ **Strength:** Repeat Monday's workout.

⊃ **Flexibility:** Repeat Tuesday's flexibility workout.

ESTIMATED CALORIES BURNED: 300

SUNDAY: CARDIO

⊃ **Steady-state workout:** Choose any cardio activity—walking, running, swimming, cycling, etc.—that you can sustain at a moderately high intensity for 50 to 60 minutes (for details, see page 170).

ESTIMATED CALORIES BURNED: 375–900

TOTAL WEEKLY CALORIES BURNED: 2,365–3,600

WEIGHT LOSS WORKOUT

Anyone who has fought the weight loss battle realizes that it's not easy. There's no supplement that will help the pounds melt off, no single exercise that will trim and tone all over. You need a recipe of regular cardiovascular training to burn fat and strength training to build lean muscle mass. The National Institutes of Health recommends doing at least sixty to ninety minutes of moderate exercise a day if your primary goal is weight loss. You won't have to do quite that much on most days, since you'll be exercising at a higher intensity, but you will need to do some type of workout almost every day. And since nutrition is a crucial part of weight loss, don't forget to follow the diet plan and tips in Chapter 14. Trainer Larry Krug explains the importance of following a low-glycemic diet and gives his recommendations and recipes for a delicious 1,500-calorie-a-day plan, with additional meals and snacks if necessary.

Elements of the Weight Loss Workout

Your scale-shifting routine will include regular cardio training (you'll do something on most days of the week), plus three weekly strength workouts and two to three flexibility sessions to stave off injury with this active plan. This is definitely an intensive program, so if you feel it's too much at any point, back off and do the beginner's routine for a few weeks to build up your aerobic base and muscular endurance. Remember to use a weight that's heavy enough to fatigue your muscles by the final rep.

WEIGHT LOSS WORKOUT PLAN

WEEKS 1–4

MONDAY: CARDIO AND FLEXIBILITY

⮕ **Cardio—interval workout, 35 minutes:** Follow the interval program on page 171 to blast calories and fat while improving your aerobic fitness.

⮕ **Flexibility:** Do all of the stretches shown in Chapter 13 (page 186).

ESTIMATED CALORIES BURNED: 575–675*

TUESDAY: STRENGTH AND CARDIO

⮕ **Strength:** Do 2 to 3 sets, 13 to 15 reps per set, of each of the following exercises:

▶ Band series (page 84; works arms, chest)

▶ Stability ball incline plank (page 83; works arms, chest)

▶ Back extension on ball (page 118; works back)

▶ One-arm cable row with rotation (page 113; works back)

▶ Anterior and lateral dumbbell T-raise (page 101; works shoulders)

▶ Rear delt dumbbell fly (page 102; works shoulders)

▶ Reaching lunge (page 153; works legs, butt)

▶ Butt blaster (page 159; works butt)

▶ Ball squat (page 139; works legs, butt)

▶ Rotational step-up (page 146; works legs, butt)

▶ Bent-knee hundred (page 124; works abs)

▶ Plank pull (page 131; works abs)

⮕ **Cardio—steady-state workout:** Choose any cardio activity (walking, running, swimming, cycling, etc.) that you can sustain at a moderately high intensity for 30 to 40 minutes (for details, see page 170).

ESTIMATED CALORIES BURNED: 500–870

WEDNESDAY: CARDIO AND FLEXIBILITY

⮕ **Cardio—interval workout, 35 minutes:** Follow the interval program on page 171 to blast calories and fat while improving your aerobic fitness.

⮕ **Flexibility:** Do all of the stretches shown in Chapter 13 (page 186).

ESTIMATED CALORIES BURNED: 575–675

THURSDAY: STRENGTH AND CARDIO

⮕ **Strength:** Repeat Tuesday's workout.

⮕ **Cardio—steady-state workout, 30–40 minutes.**

ESTIMATED CALORIES BURNED: 500–870

FRIDAY: OFF

SATURDAY: CARDIO/STRENGTH CIRCUIT

Follow either the no-weight or weight option circuits on pages 172–181 to burn fat while sculpting all your major muscle groups.

ESTIMATED CALORIES BURNED: 325–450

SUNDAY: STRENGTH

Repeat Tuesday's workout.

Optional: Do some basic cardio on your own for 20 to 30 minutes.

ESTIMATED CALORIES BURNED: 270–720

*All calories based on a 150-pound person.

TOTAL WEEKLY CALORIES BURNED: 2,745–4,260

MONDAY: CARDIO AND FLEXIBILITY

⮕ **Cardio—interval workout, 35 minutes:** Follow the interval program on page 171 to blast calories and fat while improving your aerobic fitness.

⮕ **Flexibility:** Do all of the stretches shown in Chapter 13 (page 186).

ESTIMATED CALORIES BURNED: 575–675

TUESDAY: STRENGTH AND CARDIO

⮕ **Strength:** Do 2 to 3 sets, 10 to 12 reps per set, of each of the following exercises:

▸ Diamond push-up with medicine ball (page 82; works arms, chest)

▸ Bridge chest press (page 89; works arms, chest)

▸ One-arm dumbbell row plus lunge (page 112; works back, legs, butt)

▸ Overhead press (page 117; works back, shoulders)

▸ Anterior pull (page 96; works shoulders)

▸ Seated one-arm pull (page 104; works back, shoulders)

▸ Twisting lunge (page 154; works legs, butt)

▸ Staggered squat (page 156; works legs, butt)

▸ Hip bridge (page 140; works butt)

▸ Romanian dead lift (page 144; works legs, butt)

▸ Tuck slide (page 125; works abs)

▸ Roll-up with ball (page 126; works abs)

⮕ **Cardio—steady-state workout:** Choose any cardio activity—walking, running, swimming, cycling, etc.—that you can sustain at a moderately high intensity for 45 to 50 minutes (for details, see page 170).

ESTIMATED CALORIES BURNED: 610–1,020

WEDNESDAY: CARDIO AND FLEXIBILITY

⮕ **Cardio—interval workout, 35 minutes:** Follow the interval program on page 171 to blast calories and fat while improving your aerobic fitness.

⮕ **Flexibility:** Do all of the stretches shown in Chapter 13 (page 186).

ESTIMATED CALORIES BURNED: 575–675

THURSDAY: STRENGTH AND CARDIO

⮕ **Strength:** Repeat Tuesday's workout.

⮕ **Cardio—steady-state workout, 45–50 minutes.**

ESTIMATED CALORIES BURNED: 610–1,020

FRIDAY: OFF

SATURDAY: CARDIO/STRENGTH CIRCUIT

Follow either the no-weight or weight option circuits on pages 172–181 to burn fat while sculpting all your major muscle groups.

ESTIMATED CALORIES BURNED: 325–450

SUNDAY: STRENGTH

Repeat Tuesday's workout.

Optional: Do some basic cardio on your own for 20 to 30 minutes.

ESTIMATED CALORIES BURNED: 270–720

TOTAL WEEKLY CALORIES BURNED: 2,965–4,560

MONDAY: CARDIO AND FLEXIBILITY

⊙ **Cardio—interval workout, 35 minutes:** Follow the interval program on page 171 to blast calories and fat while improving your aerobic fitness.

⊙ **Flexibility:** Do all of the stretches shown in Chapter 13 (page 186).

ESTIMATED CALORIES BURNED: 575–675

TUESDAY: STRENGTH AND CARDIO

⊙ **Strength:** Do 2 to 3 sets, 8 to 10 reps per set, of each of the following exercises:

▶ Horizontal pull-up (page 81; works arms, chest)
▶ Overhead triceps extension on ball (page 90; works arms)
▶ Lat extension (page 114; works back)
▶ High band row (page 115; works abs, back)
▶ Standing cross-country skiing with band (page 97; works shoulders)
▶ One-arm cross-band lateral (page 98; works shoulders)
▶ Side lunge (page 155; works legs, butt)
▶ Single-leg hip bridge (page 158; works butt)
▶ Split squat (page 141; works legs, butt)
▶ Calf raise (page 147; works legs)
▶ Around the world (page 127; works abs)
▶ Three-part crunch combo (page 129; works abs)

⊙ **Cardio—steady-state workout:** Choose any cardio activity—walking, running, swimming, cycling, etc.—that you can sustain at a moderately high intensity for 50 to 60 minutes (for details, see page 170).

ESTIMATED CALORIES BURNED: 645–1,170

WEDNESDAY: CARDIO AND FLEXIBILITY

⊙ **Cardio—interval workout, 35 minutes:** Follow the interval program on page 171 to blast calories and fat while improving your aerobic fitness.

⊙ **Flexibility:** Do all of the stretches shown in Chapter 13 (page 186).

ESTIMATED CALORIES BURNED: 575–675

THURSDAY: STRENGTH AND CARDIO

⊙ **Strength:** Repeat Tuesday's workout.
⊙ **Cardio—steady-state workout, 50–60 minutes.**

ESTIMATED CALORIES BURNED: 645–1,170

FRIDAY: OFF

SATURDAY: CARDIO/STRENGTH CIRCUIT

Follow either the no-weight or weight option circuits on pages 172–181 to burn fat while sculpting all your major muscle groups.

ESTIMATED CALORIES BURNED: 325–450

SUNDAY: STRENGTH

Repeat Tuesday's workout.
Optional: Do some basic cardio on your own for 20 to 30 minutes.

ESTIMATED CALORIES BURNED: 270–720

TOTAL WEEKLY CALORIES BURNED: 3,035–4,860

YOUR WORKOUT QUESTIONS ANSWERED

Do you have questions about how much weight to lift? What should you do if you don't have time for every exercise in the program, or the necessary equipment to do the suggested moves? Read on for answers on these and more ways to get your optimal results.

Q: *How much weight should I use in the strength exercises that call for added resistance like dumbbells or medicine balls?*

A: For years, experts have used a standard known as 1RM, or 1 repetition max, to help exercisers determine just how much weight they should be lifting. As you might guess, 1RM is the heaviest weight you can safely lift in an exercise without breaking form. But since it can be difficult, and even dangerous, to try to determine 1RM, more recently other experts recommend something called repetition maximum zone testing, which involves determining how much weight you can lift safely without breaking form in a wider range of reps. This method is much more direct: simply choose a weight that is heavy enough for you to lift no more than fifteen times if you're a beginner or ten to twelve times for more experienced exercisers. In other words, by the fifteenth rep (or the tenth to twelfth, depending on your experience), you should feel you cannot possibly lift the weight one more time.

Q: *Should I do the same number of reps and sets for all twelve weeks of the program?*

A: Ideally, trainers like to follow a program called periodization, which basically involves periodically varying the amount of weight and number of reps you do from week to week or month to month. At one point in the program, you may lift heavier weights with fewer reps, then lighter weights with higher reps. This type of training means you'll work different muscle fibers at different points in the program. With lighter weights, you may be working more type 2 fibers, which are responsible for muscular endurance. With the heavier weights, you'll target more type 1 muscle fibers, which are primarily responsible for power. Studies have shown that by challenging both types of muscle fibers, you'll gain more strength and sculpt more muscle.

For most of the exercises, we're recommending a range of thirteen to fifteen reps in the first four weeks of the program. That means choosing a weight that will make your muscles really feel tired by about the tenth to twelfth rep, but not so heavy that you cannot do the final rep. In the next four weeks, switch to a range of ten to twelve reps with somewhat heavier weights. And in the final four weeks, increase the weight slightly again, so that you can only lift between eight and ten reps. Most periodization programs also include a built-in rest period, so after you finish the twelve-week program, take at least one week off, doing no strength training and just a little low-impact cardio to help you recover and recharge for your next bout of training.

Q: *But if I lift heavy weights, won't that mean I'll get bulky muscles? I'm going for more of a lean, toned look.*

A: Many women are afraid that if they lift anything heavier than a paperweight, they'll get arms like a body builder. But it's almost impossible for most women to gain significant muscle mass; they simply don't have the hormonal makeup to bulk up. In fact, by challenging your muscles with heavier weights, you'll get both leaner and stronger, says trainer Joe Dowdell, who frequently puts *Sports Illustrated* swimsuit models on a high-intensity strength-training plan.

Q: *How long should I rest between each exercise?*

A: It depends on your goals, says trainer Christel Smith. If your primary goal is to gain strength, you'll need to take as long as three to five minutes. But for the majority of us, who simply want to shape and tone, the ideal rest amount is forty-five seconds to one minute. Some trainers recommend varying your rest time as part of your periodization program, since a shorter rest time can be more of a challenge to your muscles. In general, we recommend sticking to the forty-five-second rule, but if you're lifting heavier weights and feel like you need a little more time, then take an extra minute or so to get your bearings.

If that seems like an unbearably long time when you're in a rush to get your workout over and done with, you can speed things up by working different muscle groups back to back. In other words, if you start with a chest exercise like a push-up or chest press, follow it with a back move like the dumbbell row. This way, you'll rest one muscle group (the pectorals) while working another (the upper back). Or move from an upper-body exercise, like a band pull, to a lower-body move like a ball squat. This technique, pairing two or more exercises without resting, is known as super setting, and it's a great way to speed up your workout and also blast more calories, since you'll keep your heart rate elevated longer.

Q: *How should I begin my workouts?*

A: Before every workout, take just a few minutes to warm up with some light cardio activity. This will prepare your body for the work to come, increase blood flow to the working muscles, elevate your heart rate slightly, and raise your body temperature. Go for a five-minute walk on the treadmill or around the block, hop on a stationary bike, or even just march in place for a few minutes.

Q: *How do I know if I'm exercising at the right intensity?*

A: In your strength workouts, be sure to choose a weight that fully fatigues your muscle by the last rep of the set. In other words, you should feel as if you could not possibly lift the weight one more time. In your cardio workouts, follow your rate of perceived exertion, or how difficult the exercise feels on a scale of 1 to 10 with 1 being the easiest (like lying in bed) and 10 the most challenging (an all-out sprint, as if someone were chasing you). For more on determining the right effort level, see trainer Jeanette Jenkins's cardio workout in Chapter 12.

Q: *I feel kind of sore after my workout. Is it OK to skip a day?*

A: It's OK to feel some mild muscle soreness, especially the day following a strength routine. That's because muscle soreness is actually your body's way of getting stronger: When you challenge your muscles through strength training, you're creating microtears in your muscle fibers. The by-products of this training, or waste products, flood into these small tears, which experts speculate causes the muscle soreness. Rebuilding these fibers is what makes them stronger and creates muscle hypertrophy, or size. It takes some time (about twenty-four hours) for the muscles to rebuild, which is why most experts advise against strength training the same muscle groups two days in a row. If you feel mild soreness after a cardio workout, it might just be your body's way of getting used to a new type of exercise. However, if you are feeling joint pain or the exercise itself feels uncomfortable, cross-train with a different type of low-impact workout like walking, cycling, swimming, or using the elliptical

THE A-LIST WORKOUT PLANS

machine. And if you still feel excessively sore forty-eight hours after your work-out, it's probably safer to do either a much lighter version of your original plan or something more moderate, like taking a brisk thirty-minute walk. Skipping one or two workouts won't make a dramatic difference to your progress, and it's safer than risking injury. To combat soreness, ice the affected area after exercise, do some light stretching, and follow a particularly hard workout with light cardio on the day after.

Q: *I have a history of joint injuries. Is it safe for me to do these workouts?*

A: If you have any previous history of joint injuries, such as knee, ankle, elbow, or hip problems, as well as lower-back pain, you should check with your doctor before engaging in an exercise program. Many of the workouts featured in this book are intense and should be approached cautiously. However, that's not to say that exercise is off your must-do list for good: many of the moves can be modified to suit different fitness levels and accommodate special needs. For example, during a squat exercise, don't go quite so deep, especially if you have knee injuries. If your doctor clears you to exercise, follow the beginner plan and be sure to choose low-impact exercises where indicated. By incorporating strength, cardio, and flexibility exercises regularly into your program, you may be able to reduce your risk of joint pain in the future.

Q: *I'm too busy to do all the workouts in my plan! Is there a more moderate approach I can take?*

A: The workouts in this book are structured to achieve maximum results. There's no magic formula for getting a slim, sculpted body other than putting in the time to exercise and following a healthful diet. That said, there will almost always be times when obstacles—a busy schedule, travel, family commitments, and so on—will get in the way of your workout plan. If you can't commit to getting to the gym, try to do a modified version of the workout at home. If you're really pressed for time, try to squeeze in one of the circuit programs on pages 172–181, which can give you a combination of both cardio and strength in one workout. Too busy even for that? Grab five to ten minutes at different points in your day, and squeeze in small bouts of exercise: take a long walk around the block, sprint up the stairs instead of taking the elevator, park a little farther away from the store. Research has shown that even these small bursts of exertion over the course of the day can add up to the same benefits of a longer workout.

Q: *I don't have access to the equipment mentioned in the chapters. What should I do?*

A: As we mentioned in Chapter 4, while it's great to have a set of dumbbells or even resistance bands at home, you can still get a great workout using substitutions around the house. Things like soup cans, milk jugs, and even heavy boots can fill in for dumbbells. If you don't have a stability ball, you can substitute a chair for some of the exercises or even a large sofa cushion for others. While it's ideal to use something that will provide adequate resistance and challenge your muscles, you can make do with what you have on hand to see results.

Q: *I'm really willing to put in the time to get results. Can I skip the rest day in my plan?*

A: Your body needs adequate rest and recovery in order to get stronger. Too many days without a break will increase your risk of burnout and injury. That's why we always recommend resting at least one day a week (a little more for beginners). But rest doesn't have to mean baby-sitting the remote control for the day. A brisk walk around the neighborhood at lunch or after dinner for ten to thirty minutes can help you stay motivated and in tune with your program. Rest is just as important as your work days when it comes to getting results.

Q: *I hear a lot about proper form and posture. How do I know if I'm doing the move right?*

A: Form and posture are both essential when you're exercising, especially during strength moves. If you compromise either, you minimize results while maximizing injury risk. Remember to keep your shoulders pressed down away from your ears, your back tall, and your knees slightly soft (never locked). During exercises that are done while standing, like squats, keep your feet hip width apart and your body weight distributed over the entire surface of both feet. Also try to remember to pull your abdominals in and hold them there. A tight core will also help you balance, especially during advanced stability challenges such as using a stability ball or balance board, says trainer Christel Smith.

Breathe out on exertion (the part of the exercise that takes the most effort). Try to do your workouts in front of a mirror, so you can monitor your form, and follow the guidelines and tips the trainers have provided in each chapter.

Q: *If I'm only interested in losing weight, do I need to do a lifting program?*

A: Absolutely! Strength training is a crucial part of helping you achieve your weight loss goals. Resistance training not only burns extra calories, but by building this lean muscle mass while dropping body fat, you're also stoking your body's fat-burning engine. You've probably heard the statement that muscle burns more fat at rest (about 50 to 60 calories per pound) than fat. By adding lean muscle, your body will be burning more calories all day long. This faster metabolism will help you achieve your weight loss goals more quickly.

Q: *If I exercise, do I really need to diet?*

A: If your goal is to tone up or conquer a specific trouble zone, or if you're a beginner, you should still follow the healthy diet tips given in Chapter 14. However, you probably don't need to follow the specific recipes and meal plans given by trainer Larry Krug. If you do have weight loss as a goal, staying on these somewhat calorie-restricted diets will be crucial to your long-term success. A healthful diet and a solid exercise plan go hand in hand when it comes to achieving lasting fat loss.

Q: *Can I lose weight in one area, like my abs?*

A: As we've mentioned, it's impossible to spot-reduce in one specific body part, like a jiggly middle. That's because your body doesn't discriminate when it comes to losing weight; it draws from fat stores all over the body. You can, however, tone a specific area with targeted strength exercises, which will help you build lean, sexy muscles where you want them most. In our trouble-spot workout plan, we combine cardio exercises to burn fat everywhere with a variety of strength moves meant to firm up your upper body, abs, or legs and butt.

Q: *Will doing cardio like running or stair climbing bulk up my legs?*

A: It shouldn't. Most of us just aren't genetically programmed to build bulk from general cardiovascular exercise, unless we are going at an extremely high intensity or resistance level. However, if you are worried about bulk, try cross-training with a variety of cardio activity each week: use the stair climber machine or walk one day, then use the elliptical machine or a stationary bike during the next workout. By varying your routine, you'll work different muscle groups in your lower body, giving you a lean, balanced look. Better yet, do a circuit workout where you do ten minutes on each type of machine in one workout (for example, ten minutes each on the treadmill, climber, elliptical, and bike). It'll also help keep you motivated and reduce boredom, since you'll constantly be switching from one exercise to the next.

THE WORKOUTS

2

ALLURING ARMS AND CHEST

RICHARD HELENE GUZMÁN

6

ALLURING ARMS AND CHEST

TRAINERS: Rich and Helene Guzmán

WHEN YOU LOOK at some of the hottest actresses in Hollywood today, you'll see they have one thing in common: lean, toned, shapely arms. Whether they're on the red carpet or off camera sipping a latte, these women are not afraid to show a little muscle. And why shouldn't they? Sculpted arms look sexy. Our clients—who have included some of the biggest names in the business over the years, from Sheryl Crow to Hilary Swank—know that most women simply won't develop bulky muscle. In fact, with the right training emphasis, lifting weights will help you develop an upper body that will look great in any outfit, from tank tops to cocktail dresses.

Because most women have significantly less body fat in their upper bodies, the arms are one of the first places you'll see results when you begin an exercise program. The front of the arms, the biceps, is sometimes called the "show me" muscle because it's so quick to respond to change—so you'll see it popping when you flex it in front of the mirror.

The back of the arms, the triceps muscle group, tends to be more of a problem area for many women. From a purely functional point of view, that's because most of our daily activities are more biceps oriented. Lifting and carrying groceries in from the car, picking up a child, even drinking a cup of coffee all make heavy use of the biceps, which are a flexing muscle, meaning it comes toward the body. In contrast, the triceps muscles are extensors, meaning they move away from the body. The triceps are also more likely to fall victim to the effects of time and gravity, so many women develop a flabby upper arm as they approach middle age.

To get lean, defined arms, you need to target both the biceps and triceps muscle groups. While it's easy to work these muscles through isolation exercises like biceps curls and triceps extensions, we prefer to train our clients with multijoint movements. This means that more than one joint (such as your elbow or shoulder) is being brought into action with each exercise. The movement is more functional; you rarely move just one joint in real life. When you're carrying those groceries in from the car, you're engaging many muscle groups simultaneously. In addition, exercises that work multiple muscles and joints at the same time have the advantage of burning more calories.

With this in mind, we've designed most of the exercises in this chapter to strengthen both the arms and chest, or pectorals. Think of it as getting more bang for your buck: while you're firming your chest muscles, you'll also be getting a great arm workout, especially for the triceps. And don't forget that while strong pectorals don't mean a bigger cup size for women, they will help prevent sagging that comes with age.

It's important to remember that women, especially, don't need to work the arms too heavily to get results. We've found, when working with our star clients, that the best results come from training with more intensity and less frequency. You need to fully work the muscles to fatigue, meaning you just can't eke out one more repetition. Only when you reach this point can the

BEST UPPER-BODY ARM-SCULPTING EXERCISES

Blast calories while sculpting your arms and shoulders with these sports and aerobic activities. Add them to your A-List Workout plan in place of your steady-state workouts or as an optional activity on off days.

ACTIVITY	CALORIES PER HOUR*
Swimming	900
Tennis (singles)	720
Tennis (doubles)	450
Basketball	405
Softball/baseball	450
Beach volleyball	720
Rowing	630
Jumping rope	900
Rock climbing	990

*All calories based on a 150-pound person.

rebuilding process occur, which is exactly when your body begins to produce the lean, sexy muscles you want.

Unless you're doing dozens of repetitions—which is a waste of time and energy—you won't really reach this important point of muscular fatigue by using very light weights for the arms and chest. That's why we encourage our female clients to use heavier weights. Hilary Swank, Poppy Montgomery, and other actresses who have trained with us know that they have to work hard to see results—and they are living proof that muscles can, indeed, be attractive.

ANATOMY OF THE ARMS AND CHEST

There are three main muscle groups in each arm and two main groups in the chest. The biceps run along the front part of the upper arm. They are a two-headed muscle group that works to bend the elbow (flexion) and turn the palm toward the ceiling (supination). The triceps are a triangular-shaped set of three

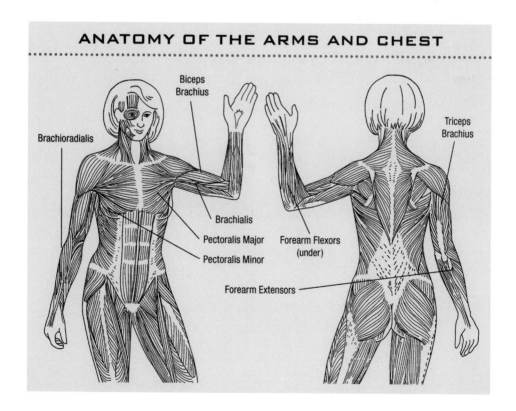

ANATOMY OF THE ARMS AND CHEST

Biceps Brachius

Brachioradialis

Triceps Brachius

Brachialis

Pectoralis Major

Pectoralis Minor

Forearm Flexors (under)

Forearm Extensors

muscles along the back of the arm and are involved whenever you use your shoulders or chest in pressing or pushing movements. And the brachioradialis is a smaller group of muscles that run along the forearms and are responsible for bending and straightening the wrists. The pectoral muscles span the upper chest and are mostly responsible for pushing and throwing movements. The pectoralis major is the primary muscle targeted in many of these exercises, although the pectoralis minor, which is responsible for depressing the shoulders, also comes into play.

★ TIP: Don't make the mistake of taking on too much, too soon when you're starting a workout program; you'll risk injury and even burn out if you overdo it. Schedule just ten or fifteen minutes in the morning, and then gradually extend your routine. We advise our clients to work out in the morning before the day's distractions—work, family, and other obligations—begin to intrude. Even just a few minutes in the morning can make a difference.

THE ALLURING ARMS WORKOUT

HORIZONTAL PULL-UP

The horizontal pull-up primarily targets the biceps, although you'll also be working the shoulders, chest, and even the abdominals to help you stay stabilized. You can do this at the gym on a Smith machine or at a park on a low set of monkey bars. You can also try this at home by placing a broom handle or Body Bar across a pair of low chairs (being careful that the chairs are sturdy and that the bar does not roll forward). This move is a great alternative to push-ups for working both the chest and the biceps. The higher the bar, the more difficult the exercise is to perform.

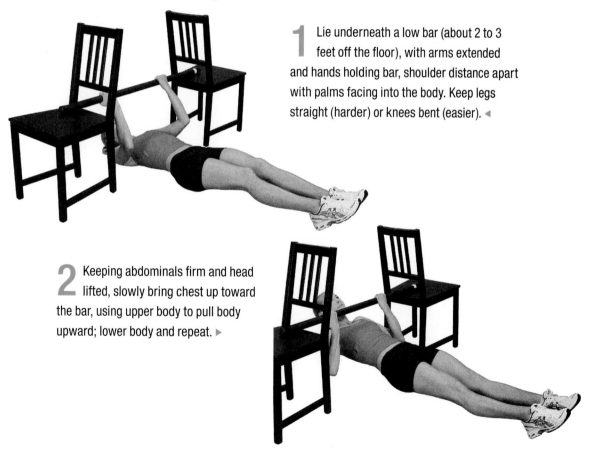

1 Lie underneath a low bar (about 2 to 3 feet off the floor), with arms extended and hands holding bar, shoulder distance apart with palms facing into the body. Keep legs straight (harder) or knees bent (easier). ◄

2 Keeping abdominals firm and head lifted, slowly bring chest up toward the bar, using upper body to pull body upward; lower body and repeat. ►

DIAMOND PUSH-UP WITH MEDICINE BALL

The diamond push-up works the triceps and the chest muscles. If you're at a gym, use a medicine ball. At home, you can use any firm ball (like a basketball) or even a small pillow. The ball provides an added challenge because you have to work to stay balanced on the rolling surface. If you sometimes suffer from wrist strain during push-ups, the ball can actually make the move easier by providing some cushioning. Beginners should do this exercise on their knees; more advanced participants can do a full push-up on their toes. If you're having trouble, try doing basic push-ups without the ball.

1 Get into a push-up position, either on knees (beginners) or with legs fully extended (advanced). Place both hands on surface of ball, touching index fingers and thumbs together to form a diamond.

2 Bend elbows, and slowly lower chest toward ball, keeping abs tight and head in line with spine. Push back up to start, and repeat.

STABILITY BALL INCLINE PLANK

Using a stability ball increases the challenge of the plank—also known as the up phase of a push-up—because your muscles have to work hard to help you stay stable. For an easier version, you can also do the exercise on the seat of a stable chair or bench. The exercise targets the chest, biceps, and triceps.

1 Kneeling on floor, place hands on stability ball about shoulder distance apart, elbows slightly bent. (If you have wrist strain, place hands closer together.)

2 Slowly roll ball forward, and raise hips until you're in a full push-up position, legs extended and arms perpendicular to floor. (To make it easier, keep forearms on ball.) Hold 5 to 15 seconds, building to 1 minute.

★ TIP: Don't lock your elbows when you're doing exercises like push-ups or triceps dips. If you do, you'll stress the joint and might cause an injury. Instead, keep your elbows soft for all exercises. That goes for knees as well when doing standing moves like squats.

BAND SERIES

Do the three exercises of the band series in order, moving from one to the next without resting in between. Use a resistance band, and do as many repetitions as it takes until your muscles feel fatigued—that is, you could not eke out one more repetition without compromising your form. This is a good series to do when you can't get to the gym. It also makes a great mini-workout for days when you can't fit in a whole routine.

> ★ TIP: During chest exercises, keep your shoulders relaxed. Often people will tense up during these exercises, compromising their form and risking injury.

PART 1: Chest Fly

1 Tie a resistance band or tubing around a sturdy object at about chest height. Stand facing away from band, holding one end in each hand, with feet staggered (one foot in front of the other, about hip distance apart). Keeping palms facing in, slowly bring ends of band together in front of chest, being careful not to lock elbows when arms are fully extended.

> ★ TIP: To work your core while exercising your upper body, add a balance element to the move. Using a stability ball, a balance board, or even just standing on one leg will engage your abdominal muscles and help you sculpt flat, sexy abs while also reducing your risk of injury in daily life.

2 Slowly bring arms back toward sides, keeping elbows slightly bent. Return to center, and repeat. ◄

3 To make this move easier, lean away from band. To make it more challenging, try balancing on one leg. ▼

★ **TIP:** It's important to have specific goals when you're training, beyond just wanting to lose weight. Your goal can be as specific as dropping five pounds before a wedding or birthday or getting sculpted for a movie role.

★ **TIP:** Get out of the gym or your home, weather permitting, and tune in to the environment. By being outside, you'll not only challenge your muscles in new ways, you'll also prevent that claustrophobic feeling that can come from spending too much time indoors.

PART 2: Triceps Extension

1 Place one end of band under ball of right foot, holding other end in right hand. Lift right arm above body, keeping elbow bent and close to right ear.

2 Slowly extend arm, keeping elbow close to head. Lower and repeat. Do as many reps as you can on right side; switch sides and repeat.

> ★ **TIP:** Find a training buddy whose abilities are similar to your own. Humans are naturally competitive, and you're likely to put more into your workout if someone else is there. And if you know someone is waiting for you, you'll also be less likely to skip your workout.

PART 3: Biceps Curl

1 Stand on center of band, with feet spaced shoulder distance apart. Hold one end of band in each hand, with palms facing up and elbows close to sides.

2 Keeping elbows pressed into rib cage, slowly curl hands toward shoulders, keeping wrists straight. Lower and repeat. ▶

3 To make this exercise more challenging, try balancing on one leg. (Stand on the leg opposite from the one you used in the chest fly.) ▼

★ **TIP:** Find a time frame that works for you. If you're a morning person, schedule your workouts in the early part of the day; if you're better later in the day, do it then. The most important thing is to be consistent. Don't throw out the whole week if you skipped one workout—instead, focus on the next session. In the long run, a single missed workout won't make a difference, but falling off the exercise bandwagon entirely will.

MEDICINE BALL PARTNER TOSS

Get a workout buddy to help you with the medicine ball partner toss. You'll need an eight- to twenty-pound medicine ball, with the weight depending on your fitness level. This move targets the biceps, triceps, and chest muscles. It's a great way to work your entire upper body. If you don't have a partner, throw the ball up above your head and catch it.

1 Stand a few feet away from partner, feet staggered with knees slightly bent, shoulders relaxed, and holding medicine ball in front of body at chest level, elbows bent and out to sides.

2 Keeping knees soft, toss ball to partner, letting ball explode further as you push it away from you. Continue tossing and catching ball as many times as you can (aiming for no more than 20 reps).

3 For an added challenge, balance on one leg as you catch and throw the ball.

★ TIP: Avoid the temptation to give in to junk food cravings. Plan what you're going to eat through the day, and have healthful choices at the ready. Fruit, cut-up vegetables, nuts, and even protein bars are good options when you're looking for something to snack on.

BRIDGE CHEST PRESS

Using the stability ball again increases the core challenge of the bridge chest press, since your abdominals must be engaged to support your body throughout the exercise. If you don't have access to a ball, you can also perform this exercise on the floor or off an ottoman or low couch. This move works the chest and biceps, as well as the deep abdominal muscles.

1 Rest head, neck, and upper back against a stability ball, holding a medium-weight dumbbell in each hand, palms facing forward. Lift hips until lower body is in a tabletop position, with hips square and glutes engaged. Extend both arms above chest, with hands shoulder distance apart. ▶

2 Slowly lower elbows out to sides, bringing weights to chest level. Return to start and repeat, keeping hips lifted throughout the exercise. ▼

> ★ **TIP:** Exhale with noise while you're lifting the weight (contracting the muscle), and inhale as you lower it (extend the muscle). You'll prevent a condition called the Valsalva maneuver, a potentially dangerous elevation of blood pressure caused when you hold your breath during an exercise. Breathing loudly forces you to relax by pushing out all the tension in your body.

3 For an advanced variation, lift one leg off the floor.

> ★ **TIP:** Order smart when you're eating out. Get a small salad as soon as you get settled, and skip the temptation to finish the bread bowl.

OVERHEAD TRICEPS EXTENSION ON BALL

For the overhead triceps extension, you can use either dumbbells or a medicine ball weighing five to fifteen pounds. By sitting on a stability ball and using just one leg as a base, you make this exercise especially challenging for the abdominals while you work the triceps. An extremely advanced athlete can try lifting both legs while lifting and lowering the weight; beginners might want to keep both feet on the floor throughout. If you do not have access to a stability ball, you can also perform the exercise on a chair or bench.

> ★ **TIP:** The finish line of a race can be a huge motivator. Sign up for an event like a local 5K a few weeks or months in advance, and then make it your goal to complete it in the best time that you can. In 2005, almost half of our clients signed up to train for the Malibu Triathlon, a half-mile swim, eighteen-mile bike ride, and four-mile run. Many went on to complete it either as individuals or in a team relay. When our clients are working on a special project, it's important for them to stay motivated, and having a goal like finishing a triathlon is a great payoff to work toward.

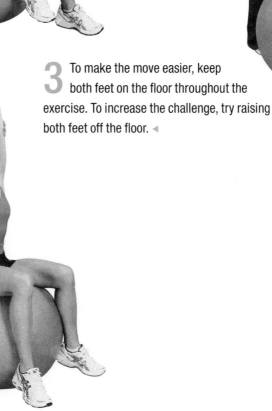

1 Sit on stability ball, holding weight or medicine ball in both hands, extending arms overhead with elbows close to ears. Keeping abs tight, lift right foot a few inches off the floor. ◄

2 Bend both elbows, bringing ball or weight behind head; keep leg lifted. Bring weight back overhead while lowering leg to floor. Repeat, this time lifting left leg while lowering ball or weight behind you. ►

3 To make the move easier, keep both feet on the floor throughout the exercise. To increase the challenge, try raising both feet off the floor. ◄

CHRISTEL SMITH SENSUOUS SHOULDERS

7

SENSUOUS SHOULDERS

TRAINER: Christel Smith

YOUR SHOULDERS are one of the body's most important muscle groups, and not just because of the way they look in the mirror. They're involved in just about everything you do, from picking up a bag of groceries to styling your hair or brushing your teeth. If you've ever played tennis or golf, swung at a ball, or gone swimming, you've given your shoulders a workout.

Of course, from an aesthetic standpoint, lean, shapely shoulders are definitely sexy. Defined shoulders not only help my celebrity clients look their best when walking the red carpet in an eye-catching strapless gown, they're also an important way to help give the body some symmetry. If you tend to keep weight in your lower body—which is where women, especially, tend to store excess fat—working your shoulders and upper back will help provide a balanced look, drawing attention away from your hips and thighs.

My female clients, who have included actresses Uma Thurman and Daryl Hannah, are primarily interested in achieving lean, toned muscles. I trained both women on the set of the Quentin Tarantino movie *Kill Bill*. That movie involved a lot of punching and sword play, which really works the shoulders. We did many shoulder-specific exercises to prepare them for the long days of stunts and shooting.

Although many experts recommend avoiding very light weights for achieving muscular definition, the shoulders are one area of exception, especially for beginners. The shoulder joint is rather intricate and fragile, and it's important to focus on doing the exercises slowly and in control with lighter weights to help reduce the risk of injury. I recommend that women, especially, start out with lighter weights and more repetitions when working the shoulders in order to improve muscular endurance while creating definition.

> ★ TIP: Because the shoulders are made up of several small groups of muscles, it's essential to warm up well before doing any upper-body exercises. Shoulder injuries can be very painful, since inflamed tissue can make it difficult to move the shoulder joint in multiple directions. I strongly believe that prevention is better than cure. Start with small, gentle arm circles, gradually swinging into bigger circles forward and then backward, to warm up before you do movements in the gym or on the sports field that involve the shoulders.

The shoulder is a multifaceted area, so the exercises in this chapter are designed to target the muscles from several angles. This has much to do with the anatomy of the shoulders. The primary shoulder muscle is the deltoid, which wraps across the top of the collarbone. It inserts in three different areas, like a triangle. The front of the shoulders, or anterior deltoid, comes into action when you lift your arms directly in front of your body. The side, or medial, deltoids get worked when you lift your arms out to either side of your body. The rear, or posterior, deltoid activates when you press something away from your body or when you draw your arms back. Therefore, pushing, pulling, and pressing movements are all required to fully develop the shoulder.

Because the shoulders have several smaller muscles, you don't need to lift a lot of weight to get results. Beginners, especially, should keep the load light. Keeping your arms straight creates a long lever; the load, or weight, is farther away from the body. This in itself is already a challenge. To make sure you're isolating the muscles, be sure to perform each exercise slowly and carefully; don't give in to momentum. Keep your elbows slightly bent and your wrists straight to prevent injuries.

ANATOMY OF THE SHOULDERS

The primary shoulder muscle, or deltoid, is the rounded area over the top of your collarbone. The deltoid has three heads that insert into the upper arm bone: the anterior (front) head, the medial (side) head, and the posterior (rear) head. A small bundle of muscles and tendons, called the rotator cuff, wraps around the shoulder joint. These smaller muscles help rotate the arm in its shoulder socket and stabilize the shoulder. The rotator cuff is made up of four muscles: the supraspinatus, the infraspinatus, the teres minor, and the subscapularis. Since these muscles are often relatively weak, they can be injured easily and are often overworked, which can be a leading cause of shoulder pain.

To get lean, shapely shoulders—and avoid injury in daily activities—I recommend doing at least one exercise each for the anterior deltoids, medial deltoids, posterior deltoids, and rotator cuff.

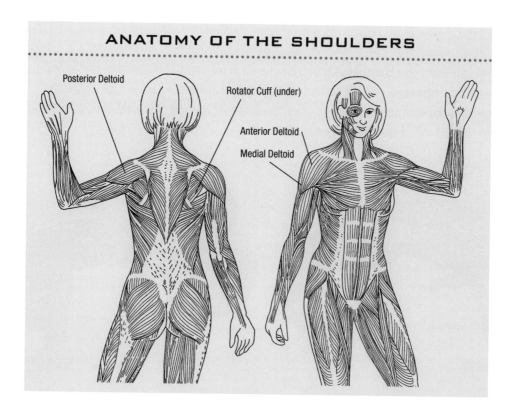

ANATOMY OF THE SHOULDERS

Posterior Deltoid

Rotator Cuff (under)

Anterior Deltoid

Medial Deltoid

THE SENSUOUS SHOULDERS WORKOUT

Anterior Delts

These exercises work the front part of the shoulders.

ANTERIOR PULL

Tie a resistance band at the base of a sturdy stationary object. Lie back on a bench facing the band, or use a stability ball to make this an abdominal-strengthening move as well. You can also do this exercise at the gym on the cable pulley machine (a staple in most health clubs). For an advanced variation, lift one foot slightly off the floor to challenge your balance.

1 Lie with upper back and shoulders on a bench or resting against a stability ball, knees bent, hips lifted, and feet flat on floor. Hold ends of resistance band in each hand with palms facing each other, thumbs up. (If you're using the cable machine at the gym, keep the attachment at your feet between your legs.)

2 Pull band or cable handles up toward your shoulders, keeping arms straight; end the movement when hands are directly over shoulders. Slowly lower and repeat.

STANDING CROSS-COUNTRY SKIING WITH BAND

For a greater challenge, tighten the tension on the resistance band or use a thicker piece of elastic. Move slowly and maintain control throughout the exercise.

1 Stand with middle of left foot on a resistance band and right foot about one step behind you. Lean forward slightly, holding one end of band in each hand, with palms facing behind you. ▶

2 Raise left hand to shoulder height in front of you while pulling right hand straight behind you. Hold 1 count; then lower and repeat, this time lifting right hand forward and left hand back. Don't use a lot of rotation in your hips; the movement should come from your shoulders. ▶▶

Medial Delts

The following exercises work the sides of the shoulders. Though the anatomical name of these muscles is medial deltoids, these exercises are often called "lateral" or side moves.

When your thumb is facing down, make sure not to bring your elbow higher than shoulder height. Raising it higher will cause impingement in the shoulders and can lead to a rotator cuff injury.

ONE-ARM CROSS-BAND LATERAL

Target the sides (lateral delts) of your shoulders with the one-arm cross-band lateral, a band-based exercise. If you're at the gym, you can do the same move on the cable machine. For an advanced challenge, do it standing on one leg, or use a balance disc or board at the gym; you can also do the exercise seated on a stability ball.

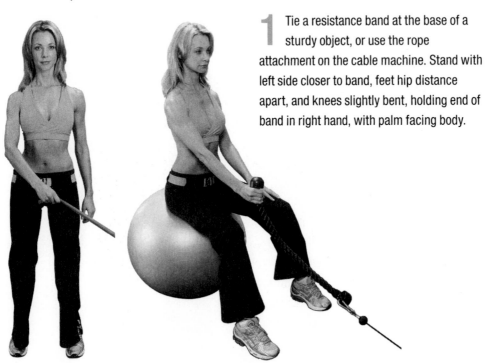

1 Tie a resistance band at the base of a sturdy object, or use the rope attachment on the cable machine. Stand with left side closer to band, feet hip distance apart, and knees slightly bent, holding end of band in right hand, with palm facing body.

2 Keeping elbow slightly bent, lift right arm out to side until it's at shoulder height. Hold 1 count; then slowly lower and repeat. Make sure not to lean sideways; stay erect as arm moves away from body.

DUMBBELL UPRIGHT ROW

When you do the dumbbell upright row, make sure you keep your shoulders down (away from your ears) so that you keep the emphasis on the delts and not the trapezius (upper back). If you suffer from any shoulder injury, eliminate this move from your routine.

1 Stand with feet hip width apart, knees slightly bent. Hold a dumbbell in each hand, palms facing body. ▶

2 Bending elbows, slowly raise weights up toward chest until they are at shoulder level with hands about shoulder distance apart. Keep elbows slightly higher than hands as you lift weights. ▶ ▶

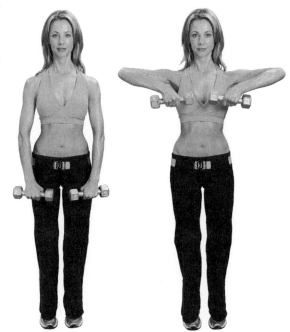

3 For an advanced challenge, try lifting one foot as you lift weights; switch legs with each set. ◀

★ **TIP:** Most women can begin with two-pound dumbbells for these shoulder exercises. When you have mastered the form, I recommend using dumbbells of about 5 percent of body weight for women and 8 percent of body weight for men. (For example, a 140-pound woman would use seven pounds, a 140-pound man between ten and twelve pounds.)

ANTERIOR AND LATERAL DUMBBELL T-RAISE

This exercise is one of my favorites, because it targets both the front and sides of the shoulders and is a great time saver if you're trying to squeeze in a quick workout. It's an advanced move, so use a very light weight.

1 Stand with feet hip distance apart, arms at sides, and palms facing behind you, holding dumbbells.

2 Lift both weights in front of you to shoulder height. Hold for 1 count.

3 Keeping arms at shoulder height, pull hands away from each other and out to the sides until they're even with chest. Hold 1 count, and slowly lower back to the start.

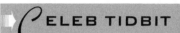

CELEB TIDBIT

Sometimes my male clients do this exercise plus a few sets of biceps curls and push-ups to look pumped just before they do a take on a film.

Posterior Delts

The following exercises work the back part of the shoulders.

REAR DELT DUMBBELL FLY

As you lift the weight, be sure to keep your shoulders down and back, away from your ears—imagine that you are trying to pinch someone's finger in between your shoulder blades. Use an incline bench (easier) or stability ball (more challenging). If you don't have a bench or ball, lie over a low stool or ottoman.

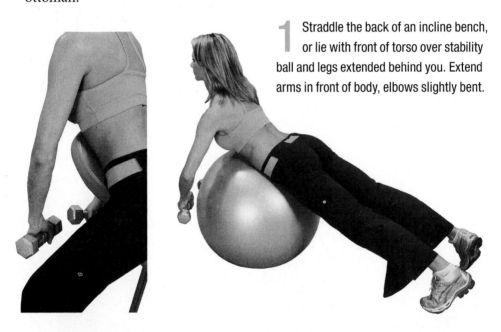

1 Straddle the back of an incline bench, or lie with front of torso over stability ball and legs extended behind you. Extend arms in front of body, elbows slightly bent.

★ TIP: Pause for a second at "peak contraction" of an exercise (the end point of the exertion phase) to make sure that you are not merely using momentum to swing the weight through. This will help ensure that you are truly contracting and isolating the muscles, which will help you see results. If you cannot hold it for more than a second, reduce the amount of weight you are lifting.

2 Lift arms directly out to sides until just under shoulder height, keeping shoulders pressed down. Hold 1 count, and then lower weights back to start.

★ **TIP:** For an advanced challenge, do a final "burn set" at the end of each exercise to really super-sculpt your muscles. This involves doing one additional set at the end of each move: Do as many reps as you can of the set. When your muscles feel fatigued (you can't do any more reps without breaking form), drop that weight, and switch to the next lighter weight. Do as many reps as you can again, and then find the next lightest weight and repeat. Follow this for as long as you can (if you're already using a fairly light weight, do the movement without any weight). Go until you can't! (Just remember to keep your form.) You will feel this!

★ **TIP:** Think of the area you are working, and "breathe" into the muscle, pausing a beat at peak contraction. You'll reduce momentum and get more out of the exercise.

SEATED ONE-ARM PULL

The seated one-arm pull is a challenging exercise that can be done at home with a resistance band (tied to a stationary object around waist height when you're seated) or at the gym on the cable machine (use the rope attachment). If you are using weights, keep the load low, as this is a difficult exercise to perform correctly. Pull the weight smoothly, without jerking your arm. To increase the challenge and work the abs, sit on a ball instead of a chair or bench.

1 Sit on a chair, bench, or ball facing band or cable with knees bent, feet planted on the floor, and torso erect. Grasp band or rope in right hand with palm facing in and left hand on left thigh for support.

2 Keeping elbow slightly bent, pull band or handle out and away to your side in a semicircular movement to shoulder height or slightly higher. Slowly return to start. Do all reps on right side, and then switch sides and repeat.

⭐ TIP: To challenge your muscles, add a slight explosive element when performing the positive part of the exercise (when you're actively pushing or pulling the load). Try to lift the weight up in one count, then hold one count, and lower in two counts. Make sure the negative phase (when you're returning to starting position) is performed slowly.

⭐ TIP: Remember to breathe throughout each exercise, both when you're lifting and when you're lowering the weight. Uma Thurman is a big yoga fan, and this really helped her get the idea of "breathing into the muscle." By focusing on the body part you are working on through a steady flow of breath, you'll fully work the target muscle.

Rotator Cuff

The following exercises target the small group of muscles that make up the rotator cuff. It's important to strengthen these muscles to prevent injuries. Although these exercises aren't specifically listed in the twelve-week program, it's a good idea to add them to your workout once a week to help keep you strong and healthy.

EXTERNAL ROTATOR BAND CURL

Make sure you keep your upper arm and elbow pressed directly into your side throughout the external rotator band curl. Maintain adequate tension with the band. You'll feel this in the outside of your shoulder and upper back.

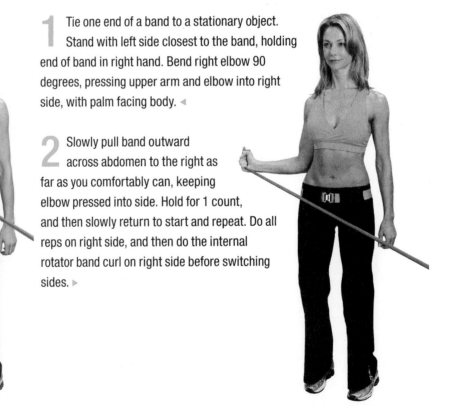

1 Tie one end of a band to a stationary object. Stand with left side closest to the band, holding end of band in right hand. Bend right elbow 90 degrees, pressing upper arm and elbow into right side, with palm facing body. ◂

2 Slowly pull band outward across abdomen to the right as far as you comfortably can, keeping elbow pressed into side. Hold for 1 count, and then slowly return to start and repeat. Do all reps on right side, and then do the internal rotator band curl on right side before switching sides. ▸

INTERNAL ROTATOR BAND CURL

The internal rotator band curl begins the same way as the external rotator band curl, except that you hold the band in your left hand with your left side closest to wherever the band is tied. To make the exercise more difficult, stand on a balance board. Keep your shoulders down, away from your ears.

1 Stand with left side closest to band, holding end of band in left hand, with left elbow bent 90 degrees, keeping forearm near abdomen, palm facing forward. ◄

2 Pull band to the right toward abdomen, moving across one even plane and ending with palm against abs. Hold 1 count, and return to start. Do all reps on left side before switching sides to do external rotator band curl with left arm. Keep elbow near waist. ▶

★ **TIP:** If you do any sport involving the upper body, whether it's golf, tennis, softball, swimming, or volleyball, be sure that you do strength exercises for your shoulders. The shoulder joint moves through a wide range of motion and often deals with quick, sudden movements, making it vulnerable to injury. Do these exercises at least once a week.

MIKE ALEXANDER A STRONG, SEXY BACK

8

A STRONG, SEXY BACK

LOOK AT YOURSELF for a moment in the mirror. Are your shoulders hunched up? Does your back round forward? Do your abs pooch out? Now think about what it means to have good posture: Stand tall, with the crown of your head reaching toward the ceiling. Press your shoulders down, and lift your chest. Engage your abs, pulling your navel in toward your spine.

See and feel the difference? Good posture is more than just healthy—it's an immediate boost, both physically and psychologically. Some people say having good posture can make you look five pounds thinner, instantly. It's also the fastest way to look and feel more confident and aware. Look at the celebrities who walk the red carpet. In addition to their aura of glamour, they carry with them an air of self-assurance, in large part because they are holding their heads high. My clients Jessica Simpson and her sister, Ashlee Simpson, are both great examples.

I describe the importance of good posture because it so ties in to this chapter's focus, the back. Posture and your back muscles go hand in hand. Over the course of a lifetime, especially for anyone who works a desk job, many people tend to develop terrible posture. They slump forward, scrunch their shoulders up toward their ears, and round their spine. Gravity—as well as poor body mechanics—takes its toll. After several years, it simply becomes habit to naturally hunch over. And it's also one big contributor to common injuries like backaches and neck pain.

Strengthening your back muscles won't instantly reverse years of poor posture, but it will help counteract this gravitational forward pull. Strong back and shoulder muscles work together to keep you from rounding forward. A strong back will also help with the demands of daily living, whether it's carrying some heavy groceries or lifting a box off the floor. Plus you'll reduce your risk of injury from things like neck and back pain. And there's no denying that a strong, sculpted back is definitely sexy, whether you're wearing a simple tank top or an elaborate strapless gown.

★ TIP: Set realistic goals. Don't expect your body to change overnight. If you expect too much, too soon, it's likely you'll get discouraged and quit exercising altogether. Remember to progress your exercises from easiest to hardest. You have to crawl before you walk, and walk before you run. Gradually change the amount of weight you can lift or the type of exercise you do, so that your body can adapt to the demands and become stronger without risking injury.

It's also important to practice good posture when you're at the gym. With each exercise you do—here and throughout the rest of this book—check in with yourself to make sure your body is in proper alignment. Stand sideways, and take a glance in the mirror: your ears, shoulders, hips, and ankles should make a straight line.

ANATOMY OF THE BACK

From behind, your upper back is definitely the focal point of the upper body. It's what gives your body that sexy V-shape look and helps your lower half, especially your hips, butt, and thighs, appear slimmer. The primary muscle group is the latissimus dorsi (a.k.a. lats). The largest muscle in your upper body, it runs along from the outer edges of your back like a pair of wings, extending from your armpits down to your waist. At the center of your back sits the trapezius, which is sandwiched between either side of your lats. This large muscle has an upper, a middle, and a lower part and works to stabilize your head and upper body. Your rear shoulders, or posterior deltoids, work in synergy with many upper-back movements. The rhomboids (major and minor) run from the shoulder blades to the spine. They work to squeeze the shoulder blades together and help move the arms backward to assist in such movements as rowing. Finally, the most important muscle group of the lower back is the erector spinae. These muscles hold up the spine and are important in preventing lower back pain.

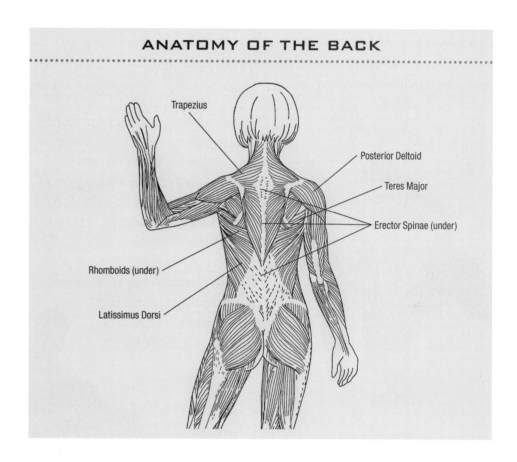

ANATOMY OF THE BACK

Trapezius

Posterior Deltoid

Teres Major

Erector Spinae (under)

Rhomboids (under)

Latissimus Dorsi

★ TIP: The key to getting great results is to keep a regular workout schedule. When Jessica Simpson was prepping for *The Dukes of Hazzard,* she worked out up to six days a week for ninety minutes a day, doing both weights and cardio, and it's one of the big reasons that her body experienced such an amazing transformation in just two months. You don't have to work out that hard or that often to get results. Give yourself six months to a year exercising at least three to four days a week. Be patient—you will see results.

THE STRONG, SEXY BACK WORKOUT

ONE-ARM DUMBBELL ROW PLUS LUNGE

The one-arm dumbbell row plus lunge works the upper back along with the legs and butt, as well as the abs. Be careful to keep your elbow close to your side as you pull the weight up.

1 Stand with feet hip distance apart, arms at sides, holding a dumbbell in right hand. Step about 12 inches forward with left foot, bending left knee 45 degrees and keeping right leg straight. Lean torso forward over front leg, resting left hand on hip; keep right arm at side with palm facing in. ◄

2 Slowly draw right elbow up behind you, keeping elbow near ribs. Hold 1 count, and lower arm. Do 12 to 15 reps; switch sides and repeat. ►

★ **TIP:** Anytime you're doing a row exercise, you'll work your biceps along with your upper back. Keep that in mind if you're combining moves from this chapter with those from Chapter 6 (alluring arms); you may have to back off on the amount of weight you are lifting for your arms if you feel fatigued.

ONE-ARM CABLE ROW WITH ROTATION

If you have a gym membership, try using the cable machine for the one-arm cable row with rotation. If you work out primarily at home, you can also replicate the exercise by tying a resistance band to a stationary object at waist height. Either way, this exercise will work your lats, obliques, and biceps.

1 Sit on a stability ball, facing the middle stack of a cable machine, holding a handle attachment in right hand, thumb facing up. (If you're using a resistance band, wrap one end around right hand, making sure you have adequate tension in the band; you can also sit on a chair.) Keep hips facing machine or band, but rotate torso slightly to the left. ▶

2 Pull right hand back, grazing elbow against rib cage. While drawing arm back, rotate torso slightly to the right, with right shoulder coming back and left shoulder moving forward. (Think about the movement of starting a lawn mower.) Slowly return to start, and repeat. Do all reps on right arm; switch sides and repeat to complete the set. ◀

LAT EXTENSION

The lat extension is a great exercise to do at home with a resistance band or on the cable machine at the gym. Tie a knot in the center of the band, and attach it in the top of a doorway, so both ends are even in length. (You can also use an attachment called a doorjamb to make the connection more secure.) Because the lats are a large, strong muscle group, be sure you have adequate tension on the band.

1 Stand facing door, holding one end of band in each hand, with center of band firmly secured through closed door. Stand back far enough that you feel tension in band, keeping arms straight in front of you at about chin height, palms down. ▶

2 Pull arms down toward sides of waist, in a V shape, keeping arms straight and shoulders pressed down. Lift arms back to start, and repeat. ▼

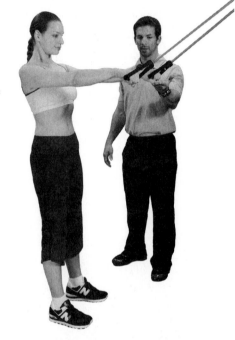

★ **TIP:** Don't exercise alone. Whether it's with a workout partner or a trainer, having someone exercise with you will make you more accountable. You'll be less likely to blow off a workout if you know someone is waiting for you.

3 As a challenge, you can hold both ends of band in one hand. You can also do this exercise at the gym on the cable machine, using the T-bar attachment.

★ TIP: Experiment with the cable machine. If you belong to a health club, you've probably seen the cable machine on the weight room floor. This highly versatile piece of equipment works nearly every muscle in the body. I like to use it for back moves, because it offers more variety than typical dumbbell exercises and allows you to work the muscles from different angles for better sculpting results.

HIGH BAND ROW

You can sit on a chair, bench, stability ball, or even on the floor for the high band row. Using a stability ball will make the move challenging for your abs; a chair or bench will provide more stability and support. Sitting on the floor will increase the range of motion for the exercise, making it more challenging for your back. Begin as for the lat extension, with the middle of the band secured at the top of the doorway.

1 Sit facing door, holding one end of band or one handle in each hand, thumbs pointing up. Make sure to be far enough away from door that there is some tension in band. Raise arms in front of you to slightly higher than shoulder height, palms facing each other. ▶

2 Lean back slightly, and draw elbows back and behind body, toward rib cage, keeping arms close to sides. Hold 1 count; slowly return to starting position, and repeat. You can also use the cable machine at the gym with the handle attachment, sitting on a bench or ball. ▼

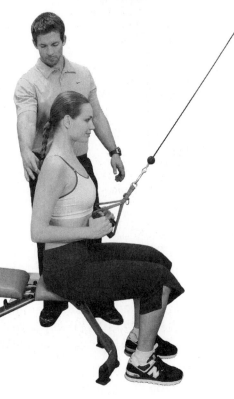

OVERHEAD PRESS

When you do the overhead press, a classic dumbbell exercise, you'll work your trapezius muscles along with your shoulders. When Jessica Simpson and I started working together, she told me she was worried about over-developing her back muscles, but by doing a smart mix of exercises, she was able to sculpt a strong, sexy back—not a bulky one.

1 Stand with feet hip distance apart, holding medium-weight dumbbells in both hands. Raising arms to shoulder height, bend elbows 90 degrees, with hands up and palms facing forward.

2 Slowly lift weights toward each other, arcing them above head; keep shoulder blades pressed down and abs tight. Hold 1 count at top of movement; slowly lower back to start, and repeat. You can also do this exercise seated on a ball. For an added challenge, lift one arm at a time.

★ TIP: Be sure to do some exercises with just one arm at a time. Most people have some bilateral weaknesses, meaning they are stronger on one side than the other. By forcing both sides to work equally, you'll reduce this discrepancy and increase your overall strength.

TIP: When I trained Jessica Simpson for her role as Daisy Duke in *The Dukes of Hazzard,* I set up a gym in a garage near the set of the film in Baton Rouge. It was challenging to find new exercises to work the back muscles, so to break up the monotony, we did a lot of exercise combinations, like doing squats and rows at the same time. It kept up Jessica's interest in the workouts and saved time by working several muscle groups together.

BACK EXTENSION ON BALL

Using a stability ball with the back extension works your abdominals along with your back, because your abs have to engage to keep you from rolling off the ball. This is a good exercise to work your erector spinae, or lower-back muscles.

1 Lie facedown on top of ball, with fingertips and toes on floor.

2 Keeping feet on floor, lift arms, bringing hands behind head or on lower back for support. Lift head, neck, and chest off ball as one unit, being careful not to overarch neck or upper back. Hold 1 count, and then lower back to a neutral position (head in line with spine). Repeat.

To make the exercise more challenging, keep hands lifted, with elbow near ears.

9

FLAT ABS, FIRM CORE

TRAINER: Teddy Bass

LAT, FIRM ABS are more than just sexy: a strong core—which includes both the abdominals and lower-back muscles—is key to feeling good and performing at your best. Of course, looking great in a bikini also is a strong motivator for most women, including many of my clients.

But there's more than just swimsuit season to think about when working your abs. The core is the center of your body; it holds everything together. Almost every movement stems from your core, whether you're picking up a piece of paper off the floor or reaching up to a shelf in your closet. If you play sports like tennis or golf, a strong core will help you generate power; if you're a runner, it will give you better speed. And if you sit at a desk most of the day, it will help prevent low-back pain and other injuries. For some of my celeb clients—including Paris Hilton, Christina Applegate, and Lucy Liu—a strong, sexy middle is important in everything they do, whether it's performing stunts in a movie or just looking good in front of the cameras.

Most of the exercises in this chapter are designed to work all of your abdominal muscles, not just the visible "six-pack" rectus abdominis, but also your deep abs (transversus abdominis), obliques, and even your lower back. By strengthening all of these muscles, which wrap around the lower torso like a girdle, you'll get a lean, defined middle that looks good and works even better. Also, it's important to think about more than just crunches when it comes to firming your midsection. Crunches are great for targeting the six-pack, but if you do only this exercise, you'll miss out on a big part of the ab-toning equation. When you're bending down to pick up an object or turning to one side, you're engaging your abdominals in several planes of motion. To keep your body strong and injury free, it's important to work in these multiple directions during ab exercises as well.

Along with gym-based moves like crunches, many of my favorite abdominal exercises also incorporate elements of Pilates. Designed in the 1920s by German innovator Joseph Pilates, these exercises focus on strengthening and toning the deep core muscles. One cue you'll frequently hear with Pilates is to "pull your navel in toward your spine." To do this, think about trying to zip up a tight pair of jeans. By doing so, you are engaging the deep transverse abdominals. The end result: a flat, firm middle.

> ★ TIP: Doing even dozens of basic crunches won't get you flat abs; that exercise is only part of the puzzle. To get results, you need to follow a well-rounded routine, targeting both the deep and superficial abdominal muscles.

The exercises here will also help keep you stable in other activities. If you strengthen the core, you'll be better able to hold your body in position, whether it's running on the treadmill or lifting a weight above your head. They'll also isolate the muscles and make them stronger for their daily function.

A few of the moves here involve a small, inflatable ball (like a children's gym ball or even a volleyball, basketball, or soccer ball) or a light medicine ball, although you can still perform the exercises without any equipment if you can't find a ball to use. I like to use the ball with my clients both as a visual cue and a challenging prop. Clients can follow their movements better by keeping their eyes on the ball, but they also have to work extra hard to keep it balanced in place during many of the moves.

The exercises in this chapter will help tighten and define the entire abdominal area. They'll improve your sports performance, reduce your risk of lower-back pain and other injuries, and even help you get more out of the other strength moves given in this book. But doing these exercises alone will not get you that eye-popping six-pack: to see that degree of definition, you must shed excess body fat by watching what you eat and burning calories through cardiovascular exercise. Combining all of these elements (diet, sculpting moves, and fat-burning cardio) will go a long way toward helping you develop the flat, sexy abs that many celebs unveil both on screen and off.

ANATOMY OF THE ABDOMINALS

The abdominals are made up of four muscle groups. The most superficial of these is the rectus abdominis, or what most people think of as the "six-pack muscle." The rectus extends vertically from the pubic bone to the sternum. It's involved in flexion, or bending forward. The deepest muscle group is the transversus abdominis, which attaches to the lower ribs and spine and encircles the entire lower torso like a corset. This muscle group is responsible for spinal support and is crucial to overall core strength. Extending diagonally along the sides and back of the body from the lower ribs to the top of the pelvic bone are the external (superficial) and internal (deep) obliques. They are involved primarily in twisting moves.

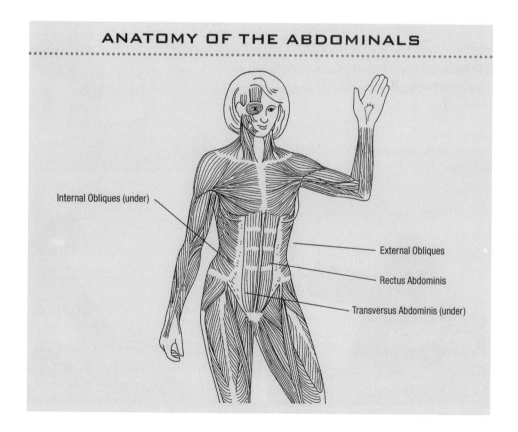

ANATOMY OF THE ABDOMINALS

Internal Obliques (under)

External Obliques

Rectus Abdominis

Transversus Abdominis (under)

THE FLAT ABS WORKOUT

BENT-KNEE HUNDRED

The bent-knee hundred is a Pilates-based move that isolates the deep abdominals, making you more aware of the muscles that you are working. Pumping your arms during the exercise increases heart rate and blood flow, making it the perfect way to start your abdominal workout.

1 Lie faceup on the floor, with knees bent 90 degrees and pulled toward chest, and arms extended above shoulders, palms facing knees. ▶

2 Lift head, keeping neck neutral and chin tucked. Extend arms along sides, and "pump" arms by lifting and lowering palms about 2 inches up and down from the floor. Inhale fully for a count of 5 pumps; then exhale for another 5 pumps. Continue pulsing arms, and follow this breathing pattern, counting to 100. Keep abdominals pulled in throughout the exercise. ▼

3 To increase the intensity, straighten the legs, keeping them on about a 45-degree angle to the floor. ▶

TUCK SLIDE

The tuck slide uses a small inflatable ball or light medicine ball, although you can still get some benefit out of doing the move without any props. Keeping the ball in place with your elbows and legs forces you to incorporate more of your abdominal muscles, giving you a more challenging variation to the standard bicycle crunch.

1 Lie faceup on floor, holding a small ball in both hands, legs extended. Lift head, neck, and shoulders off the floor, and bring knees in toward chest. Bend elbows together, balancing the ball between elbows and knees. ◄

2 Keeping upper body lifted and abs pulled in, slowly slide ball toward left knee, turning right shoulder toward left leg; at the same time, straighten right leg. ►

3 Return to center; repeat, this time moving ball toward right knee while straightening left leg. Repeat, moving ball from side to side. ◄

> ★ **TIP:** Don't just go by a scale. So many people focus on weight, and that's tangible, but the best way to judge is how your clothes feel.

ROLL-UP WITH BALL

The roll-up with ball is a very challenging move that engages the obliques, rectus abdominis, and transversus abdominis. The slower you go, the more difficult the exercise.

1 Lie faceup with knees bent 90 degrees and feet planted on floor, holding ball over head between both hands, arms extended near ears. ◄

2 Slowly lift head, neck, shoulders, and upper back, bringing ball overhead and toward the legs; keep abdominals pulled in toward spine. Hold 1 count, pressing ball forward.

3 Reverse position, and slowly roll back, one vertebra at a time, toward the floor, bringing ball back past ears and above head. Do 5 to 6 reps total. To increase the challenge, extend one leg off the floor at a 45-degree angle. For an even more advanced variation, keep both legs 45 degrees off the floor, and roll the ball toward toes at top of movement. ▼

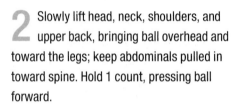

AROUND THE WORLD

"Around the World" is a Pilates-based exercise that engages all of the abdominals, especially the obliques. Focus on moving slowly and with control, using your whole torso.

1 Lie faceup on the floor with knees bent, feet flat on floor, and hands behind head with elbows out to sides. Bend left knee, crossing left ankle over right knee. Lift shoulders as high as possible, bringing left elbow and shoulder toward right knee. ▶

2 Return to center, and crunch up, keeping left ankle on right knee. ◀

3 Lower back to start, and repeat, this time bringing right shoulder toward left knee. Continue, moving from right to left with each rep. Repeat for the given number of reps, and then switch legs and repeat, moving from left to right. ▼

★ **TIP:** Ab exercises are the last thing that most people want to do in their workouts. Your best bet is to eliminate the temptation to cut the moves out by doing them either first thing or between other exercises, creating small circuits.

FAVORITE AB DEVICES

Late-night TV broadcasts are filled with fitness infomercials promising to give you flat abs with the touch of a button—or at least the quick-and-easy help of a tummy-toning fitness device. The truth is, most of this equipment gives only your wallet a workout. But there are a few fitness gadgets that can help you shape a sexy middle. Here are a few of my favorites:

⊘ **Foam rollers:** These devices, which have their roots in physical therapy, are like an oversized pool noodle. Most are about three feet long and six inches in radius, and they're a great way to improve balance, flexibility, and core strength. Lie on a roller to do basic moves like crunches; place it under your hands or feet as an extra balancing challenge for moves like push-ups or curls. Or just use it as a massage device to iron out some kinks in your muscles. (See Chapter 13 for more details about flexibility training with the foam roller.)

⊘ **Bosu:** This hybrid device—part stability ball, part step platform—marries form and function in a truly unique way. You can use the Bosu (now available in many health clubs and at sporting goods stores) as a balancing challenge; forcing your body to stay stable will incorporate the abdominals, even while you're working other muscle groups. Stand on it to do squats or lunges; lie on it to intensify crunches and sit-ups. You'll especially work the transversus (deep) abdominal muscles.

⊘ **Medicine balls:** They've been used by weight lifters for decades, but recently even casual exercisers are discovering the benefits of these weighted balls. Medicine balls come in several different weights, usually in kilograms; calculate 2.2 kilograms for 1 pound. They're great for power movements (throwing or catching the ball), and they provide added resistance for moves like crunches or twists.

★ **TIP:** Everyone wants to find the quickest, fastest way to lose weight, but fasting should not be one of them; it just doesn't work. You'll lower your metabolism and make shedding pounds even harder. A better strategy is to graze. Your body will learn to burn calories more efficiently if you eat small amounts throughout the day.

THREE-PART CRUNCH COMBO

The three-part crunch combo works with all of the abdominal muscles while also stretching the glutes and hamstrings.

1 Lie faceup on floor with right knee bent 90 degrees and foot lifted off floor, left knee bent with left ankle crossed over right knee. Place hands behind head, elbows out to the sides. Raise upper body, bringing right shoulder toward left knee. ▶

> ★ **TIP:** Be conscious of your calorie intake. Exercise is a great way to burn calories, but if you are eating more than you are expending, you will not lose weight.

2 At the top of the movement, lift lower back and tailbone off the floor in a reverse crunch. Be careful not to swing your hips or use too much momentum. ▶

3 Keeping upper body lifted, straighten right leg toward ceiling, and extend right arm, bringing hand toward right toes. Keep left arm behind head to support neck. Lower to start, and repeat from beginning, keeping abdominals pulled in throughout the exercise. Do all the reps on right side; then switch sides and repeat. ▸

★ **TIP:** You can't do just all cardio or all strength; you need to do a mix of both, especially if your goal is weight loss. If your aim is to lose twelve pounds in six weeks, it can happen, but you'll need to make a commitment of doing five to six days of cardio and strength training a week. And you have to make sure your goal is realistic.

★ **TIP:** Try not to overeat in the evenings. I try not to snack or eat after 9 P.M. Make a conscious effort not to eat two hours before you go to bed—your digestion slows down 65 percent when you're sleeping, which affects your metabolism. A lot of times, people won't eat a lot during the day, so when they get home, they're starving. Even my celebrity clients have to face this: they're not in a typical nine-to-five job, but they're on the go all day long, so they end up taking in more calories at night. You have to make an effort to eat a healthful breakfast, and then snack on good foods throughout the day. This way, you'll have more energy all day long.

PLANK PULL

The weight of your leg acts as added resistance in the plank pull, increasing the intensity of the exercise. Do this move in two parts: do all the leg lifts first, then all the knee pulls. If you need to, rest with your knees on the floor, or come into a child's pose (sitting back on heels with arms extended in front of you). To increase the challenge, this exercise can be done with your hands on a stability ball or Bosu.

1 Begin in a full push-up position, with palms on floor aligned under shoulders and legs fully extended. Keep shoulders pressed down, hips lifted, and back firm, forming a straight line from head to heels. ◄

FLAT ABS, FIRM CORE

2 Raise right foot to hip level; keep hips level and facing floor. Hold for 5 full counts. Rest, and then repeat 5 times (not shown). Next, pull right knee toward left shoulder; hold 2 to 3 counts. Repeat 3 to 5 times; return to center, and repeat on opposite leg, resting on knees if necessary between sides. ▶

3 For a more advanced move, keep both legs on a stability ball, and draw knees toward chest. ◀

★ TIP: The biggest challenge for a lot of my celebrity clients is getting them to adhere to a workout program while traveling. If they're in a big production schedule and are working all day or night, they still have to make time to get in exercise. Getting results takes determination and dedication.

★ TIP: Set realistic goals. If you want to lose weight, plan a reasonable end goal, and don't plan to lose more than two and a half pounds per week. Realistic goals are the most achievable. People look at celebrities like Cameron Diaz and think, "I want to have a body like that," but there's a lot of genetics involved. Hard work will pay off, but you have to be realistic about your end results. And think beyond just weight loss: plan on seeing more muscular development on your arms, or just set your goal of doing cardio three times a week for a month. Taking baby steps and setting a goal of achieving something tangible like losing a few pounds in one month will help you stay on track and reach your long-term goals.

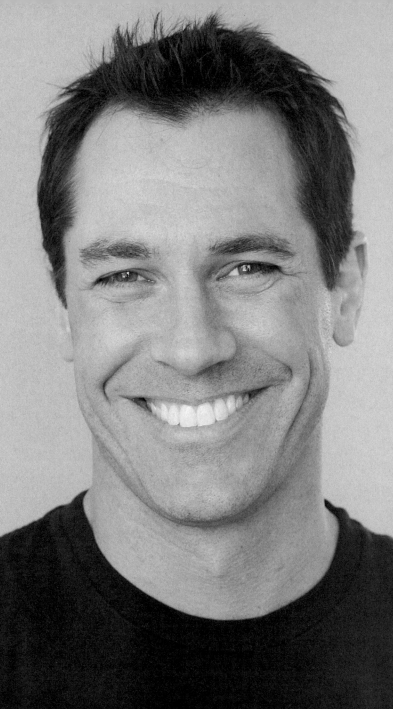

10

HEAD-TURNING LEGS

TRAINER: Joe Dowdell

S TRONG LEGS ARE SEXY. Take it from me. I train some of the world's most beautiful women, including Victoria's Secret models, *Sports Illustrated* swimsuit stars, and top film actresses such as Claire Danes, and they all have one big thing in common: a willingness to work hard.

The main leg muscles (including the quads and hamstrings) are meant to bear much of the brunt of daily movement, and they can carry your body weight and then some. One thing I tell all of my clients is that the only way to sculpt more muscle is to challenge your body—something you won't achieve by just doing lots of repetitions without much added resistance.

It takes more than just very light weights to get in shape, especially for your lower body. You have to work the muscles fully to fatigue. And while using just your body weight is a great starting point, especially for beginners, after a few weeks your body will begin to adapt, and you'll need to add more resistance to keep the muscles challenged and to continue seeing results.

The secret to my workouts is to keep intensity levels high. This has a significant effect on the hormonal system. The higher the intensity levels, the greater the release of certain hormones, such as human growth hormone (HGH). This doesn't mean you'll get bulky, especially for women. Hormones like testosterone and growth hormone are important for body composition and will help you increase lean muscle mass and decrease body fat—without bulking you up like a bodybuilder. That's because women simply lack the testosterone levels to create significant muscle bulk. Even when I'm training swimsuit models, we work at a high intensity to achieve lean muscle mass. One of my Brazilian models, who has an amazingly sleek lower body, can do a squat balancing 135 pounds of weight on her shoulders. Claire Danes does full chin-ups, pushes a machine called the sled around the gym floor, and does lots of other high-intensity, very advanced exercises.

I also prefer my clients do multijoint, multimuscle exercises, like squats, dead lifts, and lunges. This means they'll work not only the quads, hamstrings, and adductors (inner thighs), but also the glutes and core. Not only is doing these exercises a great time-saver, because you're working several muscles

CARDIO FOR SEXY LEGS

In addition to the exercises in this chapter, I recommend doing at least three energy system or cardiovascular workouts a week. Here are some of my top choices:

○ **Interval training:** Do periodic bursts of high-intensity work intervals followed by low- to moderate-intensity recovery periods, such as sprints on the treadmill or hill intervals (for more on interval workouts, see Chapter 12). With my clients, we'll vary the length, duration, intensity, and recovery time depending on where we are in our workouts. Since I have limited outdoor access with my clients, I like the treadmill, but you can also do intervals on the rower, VersaClimber, or spinning bike; all are good ways to work the leg muscles.

○ **Kickboxing:** With many of my clients, I practice kickboxing, an amazing calorie burner (more than 600 an hour) and great way to sculpt your lower and upper body. We'll skip rope, do some mitt work, hit the heavy bags, and do some light sparring, which includes throwing kicks, knees, elbows, and punches. Kickboxing is challenging, because you are working the muscles in multiple planes of movement (several directions), and a great way to get rid of some pent-up aggression.

○ **Sports and other activities:** It's important to get outside and enjoy yourself. Activities like skiing or snowboarding in the winter or in-line skating and tennis in warmer weather will give you a psychological boost in addition to a physical one.

simultaneously, it's also a good way to burn more calories in less time. Most of my celebrity clients don't have a lot of time to spend at the gym, so we try to be as economical as we can in training, which means working the most muscles possible in the shortest amount of time.

Some of the exercises that appear in Chapter 11 (great butt) also work the major muscles of the legs. Therefore, be sure to pace yourself accordingly when doing your A-List Workout plan, since you'll be targeting both the legs and butt with several of the suggested exercises.

ANATOMY OF THE LEGS

The legs are composed of several major muscle groups. The quadriceps consists of a group of four muscles that sit on the front of the thigh: the vastus medialis, vastus intermedius, vastus lateralis, and rectus femoris. The quads' primary function is to extend (straighten) the knee. Besides extending the knee, the rectus femoris also acts as a hip flexor. The quads attach at the front of the tibia (shin) and originate at the top of the femur (thigh bone), except for the rectus femoris, which crosses the hip joint and originates on the pelvis. The hamstrings run along the back of the thigh and are composed of three separate muscles: the biceps femoris (short and long head), semitendinosus, and semimembranosus. They originate just under the gluteus maximus on the pelvic bone and attach on the tibia. The hamstrings' main functions are knee flexing (bringing your heel toward your butt) and hip extension (moving your leg behind your body).

The adductors (inner thigh muscles) include the adductor magnus, adductor longus, adductor brevis, gracilis, and pectineus. They originate on the pelvic

> ★ TIP: Don't be concerned if, when you first start training, you look more bulky than lean. In the first three to four weeks, you tend to see more water retention, due to an increase in glycogen storage. Your body is storing more carbohydrates in response to your training, especially if you haven't worked at high intensity levels before. If you stay on track and drink a lot of water to prevent retention, this temporary "bulk" will go away, and you will be left with a lean, attractive look.

bone and attach at intervals along the length of the femur. Their main function is adduction, or moving the leg toward the center of the body. Finally, the lower leg muscles include those of the calf and the shin. The powerful calf muscles include the gastrocnemius and soleus, the latter of which sits deeper on the leg. Both muscles work together to elevate the heel. The anterior tibialis is the primary muscle of the shin and is responsible for elevating the toes.

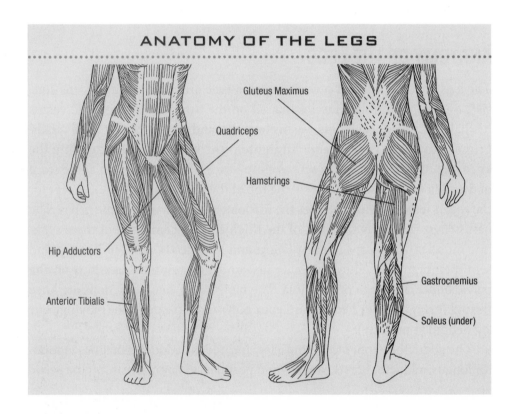

ANATOMY OF THE LEGS

Gluteus Maximus

Quadriceps

Hamstrings

Hip Adductors

Anterior Tibialis

Gastrocnemius

Soleus (under)

★ TIP: Be consistent. My training philosophy is to train smart and train hard, but most of all, be consistent. If you're just working out once a week, you're not going to reach your better-body goals. If you train hard and often but dumb, you'll end up hurt.

THE HEAD-TURNING LEGS WORKOUT

BALL SQUAT

The ball squat is a great exercise, especially for beginners. Using a stability ball behind your back adds support. As you squat, lean into the ball; it will also help you keep proper form.

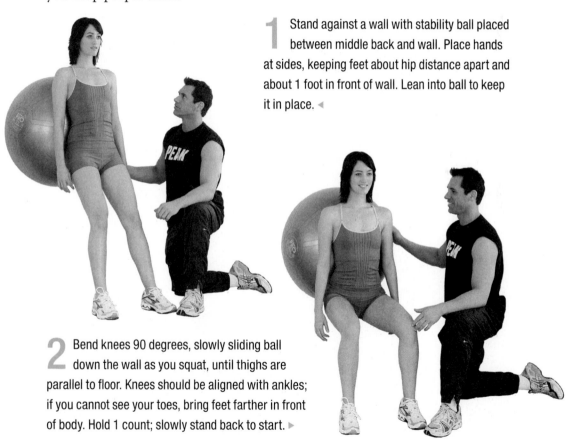

1 Stand against a wall with stability ball placed between middle back and wall. Place hands at sides, keeping feet about hip distance apart and about 1 foot in front of wall. Lean into ball to keep it in place. ◂

2 Bend knees 90 degrees, slowly sliding ball down the wall as you squat, until thighs are parallel to floor. Knees should be aligned with ankles; if you cannot see your toes, bring feet farther in front of body. Hold 1 count; slowly stand back to start. ▸

3 For a more advanced variation, hold a medium-weight dumbbell in each hand.

HIP BRIDGE

The hip bridge hits your glutes, hamstrings, and erector spinae, or lower-back muscles. To work the outer and inner thigh at the same time, try adding different props or tools, including a medicine ball and a resistance band.

1 Lie faceup on the floor with knees bent, feet flat on floor about 1 foot in front of butt. Place hands on floor, palms down. Squeezing glutes, slowly lift hips, forming a straight line from knees to waist (be careful not to overarch spine). Hold 2 counts, continuing to squeeze glutes; lower back to floor and repeat. ▶

2 To work inner thighs, hold a medicine ball or similar-size ball (for example, a soccer ball or basketball) between thighs, and squeeze legs together while lifting hips. ▶

3 To work outer hip and thighs, tie a resistance band around thighs, and press out while lifting hips. ▼

★ TIP: When models come to me with a deadline, such as getting in shape for a big event like the Victoria's Secret fashion show, I tell them to increase their activity levels throughout the day in addition to their regular workouts. That means walking around more during the day, climbing stairs instead of taking the elevator, and so on. Even small energy expenditures can add up to a lot of calories burned by the end of the day.

4 For an advanced variation, extend right leg, keeping it raised while lifting and lowering hips; switch legs halfway through the set.

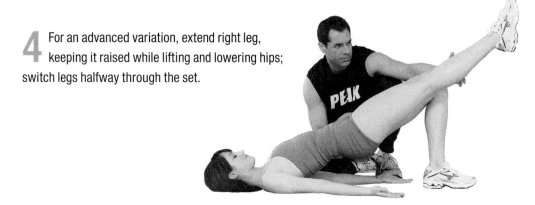

SPLIT SQUAT

Sometimes known as a stationary lunge, the split squat can be adapted to several fitness levels. Keeping your rear leg lifted makes it more of a workout for your quadriceps.

1 Stand with feet staggered, about 2 feet apart, toes pointing forward with right foot forward and left foot back. Keep torso upright, shoulders down, and arms at sides. ▶

2 Bend both knees 90 degrees, keeping right knee aligned over right ankle and left heel pointing behind you. Hold 1 to 2 counts, and come back to starting position; repeat. Do all reps on right leg; switch sides and repeat. ▼

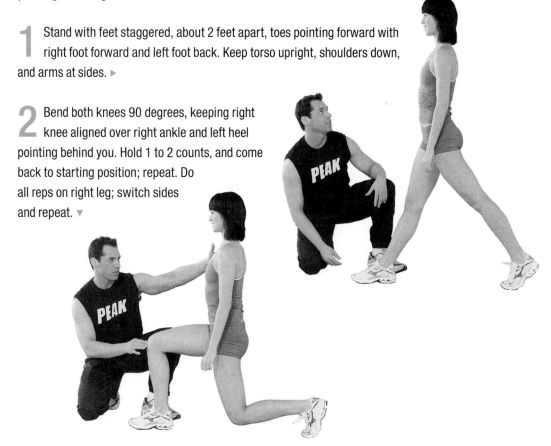

3 For an advanced variation, place top of left foot on a low chair or bench behind you, and hold dumbbells with arms at sides. For an even greater challenge, use a stability ball instead of a chair or bench (weights optional). ▶

LATERAL LUNGE

Varying your planes of movement (working from side to side rather than just front to back) is a great way to challenge your muscles and also reduce your risk of injury in and out of the gym. The lateral lunge works your inner and outer thighs, as well as your quads and glutes.

1 Stand tall with feet hip distance apart and arms at sides.

★ **TIP:** Vary your sets and reps. In addition to doing these high-intensity exercises, my clients follow a format called undulating periodization, which basically means varying the amount of work you do from week to week. Some weeks we'll do higher resistance with fewer reps and more time to rest; other times we'll do lighter resistance and more repetitions. By switching things around, you'll keep the muscles challenged and prevent a plateau in sculpting and performance. You'll follow a similar periodization-type plan in your A-List Workout, varying the amount of reps, sets, and weights every four weeks.

2 Step out to right side with right foot, bending right knee 90 degrees and keeping left leg straight. Right knee should be aligned with right toes, but body should be aligned over heels, rather than leaning forward. Keep hips facing forward and head and spine in alignment (don't round forward). Hold 1 count, return to start, and repeat. Do all reps on right leg; switch sides and repeat. ◄

3 For an advanced variation, hold a medium-weight dumbbell in each hand.

REVERSE LUNGE

Lunging behind your body, rather than forward, places less shear force on your front knee. Keep your torso upright throughout the exercise; don't lean forward or round your back.

1 Stand with feet about hip distance apart and arms at sides. ►

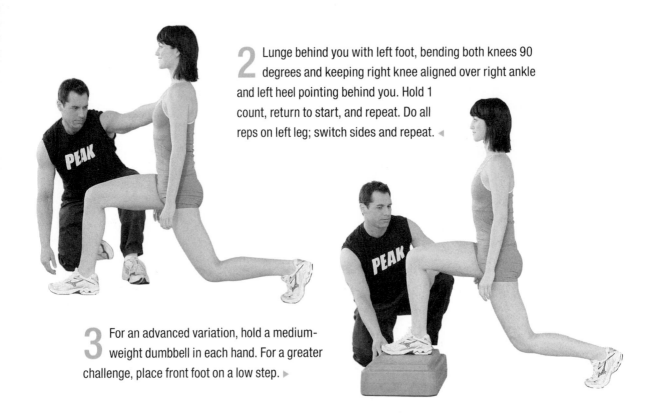

2 Lunge behind you with left foot, bending both knees 90 degrees and keeping right knee aligned over right ankle and left heel pointing behind you. Hold 1 count, return to start, and repeat. Do all reps on left leg; switch sides and repeat. ◄

3 For an advanced variation, hold a medium-weight dumbbell in each hand. For a greater challenge, place front foot on a low step. ▶

⭐ **TIP:** Take time to recover. You have to factor in recovery time when you are training, especially if you are working hard to reach a goal. If your gym has a sauna, use it after the workout; if you can afford it, get a massage once a month or every couple of weeks. Even things like alternating between hot and cold showers or taking a bath with Epsom salts to relax the muscles will help you physiologically, neurologically, and psychologically.

ROMANIAN DEAD LIFT

The Romanian dead lift is a classic strength exercise and a great way to work your lower back, glutes, and hamstrings, but it's often done incorrectly. Remember to keep your knees slightly bent and your back in a neutral position. If you start to round your spine, you've gone too far forward; bend only as far forward as you can to maintain proper form. I recommend beginners do this exercise facing a weight bench. As you bend forward, try to touch the bench with your hands. As you advance, you can go deeper and deeper into the exercise, until your torso is parallel to the floor.

1 Stand holding a medium-weight dumbbell in each hand, with palms in front of thighs and facing body. Place feet hip distance apart, and keep knees slightly bent. ▸

2 Keeping shoulders down and chest lifted, slowly bend forward, driving hips and glutes behind you while maintaining a slight bend in the knees. Keep hands close to legs, and make sure back is flat, not rounded. ▾

3 For an advanced variation, lift one leg behind you throughout the exercise. The basic movement will be the same (hinging forward from the waist), but keep your standing leg straight and extend your arms from your shoulders rather than close to your body. Hold the back of a chair for balance if necessary. ▸

ROTATIONAL STEP-UP

The rotational step-up is a challenging exercise, because you move in different planes of motion, working your hamstrings, quads, glutes, and outer-thigh (abductor) and inner-thigh (adductor) muscles. Make sure whatever you are stepping up onto is stable and can support your body weight.

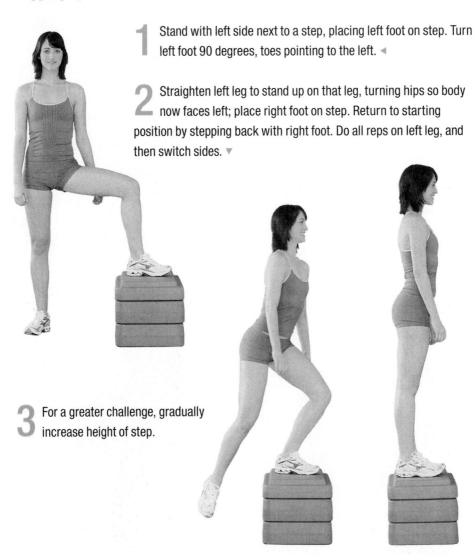

1 Stand with left side next to a step, placing left foot on step. Turn left foot 90 degrees, toes pointing to the left. ◀

2 Straighten left leg to stand up on that leg, turning hips so body now faces left; place right foot on step. Return to starting position by stepping back with right foot. Do all reps on left leg, and then switch sides. ▼

3 For a greater challenge, gradually increase height of step.

CALF RAISE

Don't forget to work your calf muscles to balance your legs and reduce the risk of injury. You don't need a lot of added weight for the calf raise; body resistance alone should be enough to help you develop the muscles.

1 Stand on a step with heels of both feet hanging over edge. ▶

2 Slowly lift up onto balls of feet, holding onto the wall or a partner in front of you for balance, if necessary. Hold 1 count at top of lift, and then lower feet until heels are just below step. ▼

3 For an advanced variation, do the move one leg at a time. ▶

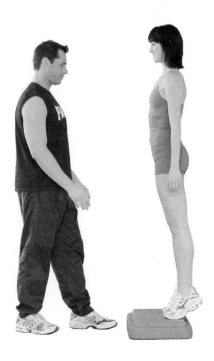

SECRETS OF A GREAT BUTT

11

TRAINER: Gunnar Peterson ▌

THERE'S NO DENYING the aesthetics of a well-developed butt. My clients are admired—and, I hope, respected—for the work that goes into their incredible physiques. Believe me, they put the time into their workouts. To keep your backyard hard and elevated, you need to work it from a number of angles, changing the intensity and types of exercise to keep the muscles stimulated.

As the body's largest muscle group, the glutes (which include the aptly named gluteus maximus, the smaller gluteus medius, and the much smaller gluteus minimus) play several roles. There's the functional one, of course: your gluteals are your primary source of locomotion, so whether you're stepping, climbing, or running, they're working. They're stabilizer muscles, too, helping you stay upright while standing in place.

The glutes are also important when it comes to helping the rest of your body look its best. Stimulating these fibers, which make up a significant percentage of your body's muscle mass, helps keep your metabolism running on high, so you'll burn more calories all day long, even when you're sitting around (call it "active rest," it sounds better!) or sleeping. The more muscle mass you have—the greater your active-to-inert tissue ratio—the more your metabolism will work for you. If you're looking to lose weight, it's crucial to include glute-strengthening exercises in your workout regimen.

Our culture, for the most part, is content to sit on its largest muscles most of the day. Unfortunately, most women tend to gain and hold their excess weight in their lower bodies, especially the hips and butt.

A common focal point among my clients is the shape or "height" of the butt. Some feel their butt is too flat. Others are concerned about building up too much muscle in their lower bodies and bulking up. They want lean glutes, not "muscley" ones (a contradiction, by definition!). And then there are those who simply seek a backside they can be proud of, whether they're wearing something revealing on the red carpet or relaxing on vacation with friends or family. A common request for many is the "bubble" butt.

To get a butt that works for you, literally *and* figuratively, you need to target all three gluteal muscles. Strengthening the maximus will hold that bubble in place; the medius and minimus contribute to that shape while also giving you that athletic look on the side of the butt. It's also important to work the muscles through a full range of motion. Targeting the top of the butt, for example, will help that "shelf" look and keep it lifted.

I believe in functional exercises—moves that work as well in real life as they do at the gym. That means doing a lot of squats and lunges while also incorporating the muscles of the upper body. These exercises more closely mirror what you do in everyday life (bending down to pick up a laundry basket, for example) *and* stimulate more muscle fibers, so you'll burn more calories in every workout.

I also like exercises that involve a balance challenge. You'll reduce your chances of falling or even jarring your joints if you've practiced working in an unstable environment. As a stabilizer, your butt is constantly being called into action, so you're always getting somewhat of a workout. Exercises on one leg or using balancing tools like a foam pad or disks are just a few ways to bring balance into the equation. You're also preparing your body to avoid injury, as much as you possibly can, in the event that you step off an unexpected curb or trip over a tree root in the backyard.

You can make these exercises harder or easier, depending on your fitness level. If you're just starting out, you can modify the moves by bending a shorter distance or skipping the dumbbells (you can hold something a lot lighter, like water bottles, which will give you the sensation of holding a weight without too much added stress). If you want a greater challenge, move a little deeper, and feel free to experiment with different-size weights. Remember that if any move feels uncomfortable or causes pain, stop and gently stretch the affected area.

ANATOMY OF THE BUTT

There are three major "butt" muscles, and it's important to target all of them to develop a fabulous rear view. The one most of us have heard of is the gluteus maximus, the large muscle that makes up the "cheek." The muscle fibers run diagonally from the midline of your butt around to the side of the hip. The job of the gluteus maximus is to straighten the leg, whether you're rising from a chair or walking forward. Whenever you push off with your leg and step forward, your maximus is doing most of the work. The maximus is also responsible for lifting the leg away from the body (toward the rear). To shape this muscle, focus on exercises that use a similar pushing-off motion.

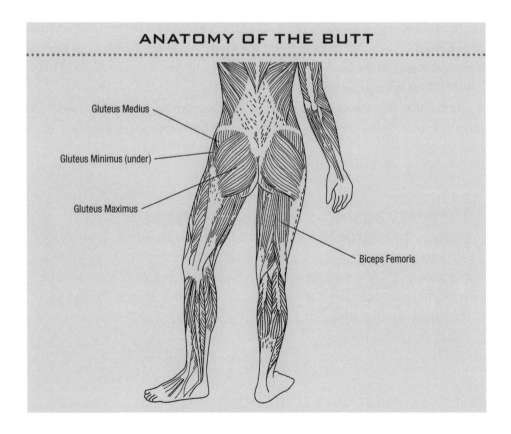

ANATOMY OF THE BUTT

Gluteus Medius

Gluteus Minimus (under)

Gluteus Maximus

Biceps Femoris

Underneath the gluteus maximus is, appropriately enough, the gluteus medius. It's situated at the upper outer hip, partially under the maximus. This slightly narrower muscle is mostly responsible for stabilization. It's what keeps you upright when you're standing or reaching. It's also used whenever you're lifting your leg out to the side or rotating it. A strong medius is important not just because you use it constantly, but also because it creates a tighter, rounder look—and in L.A., that counts for a lot! To target the medius, do exercises that bring the leg out away from the body or require you to balance on one leg or use pivoting movements.

Finally, there's the gluteus minimus. It's the smallest and the deepest of the butt muscles, positioned beneath and slightly in front of the medius. It functions in a similar way to its neighboring muscle. Most of the time that you're engaging the medius you're also using the minimus, and working the minimus will help you more fully develop your assets.

One more body part to consider when you're beautifying your backside is the back of the leg, a.k.a. the hamstrings. This muscle group, which includes the biceps femoris, runs along the back of the leg from the bottom of the glutes to behind the knee. Its job is to bend the knee. While the hamstrings are not technically part of the butt, strong hamstrings will go a long way toward helping your butt get a lifted look.

Remember that many of the exercises in Chapter 10, Lean, Sexy Legs, also target the butt. So be careful not to overdo it when performing exercises from both chapters.

★ TIP: All the strength exercises in the world won't show your work if excess body fat is covering up the muscles. To reveal the goods, you need to do moderate-intensity aerobic exercise at least four days a week for 30 minutes or longer. While most aerobic activities are good at burning calories, some do double duty by also working the glutes as they raise your heart rate. The best in the bunch include kickboxing, cycling (moderately high intensity), elliptical machines (backward setting), walking or running on an incline, and in-line skating.

THE GREAT BUTT WORKOUT

REACHING LUNGE

The reaching lunge is amazing for targeting the gluteus maximus.

1 Stand with feet together, holding a set of weights with arms at sides. ◄

2 Take a step forward with right foot (anywhere from 12 to 24 inches, depending on your height). Reach down to tap both weights to the floor in front of right foot. Keep right knee over ankle (not over toes) and hips high. The majority (85 to 90 percent) of body weight should be on front foot. Push off right foot, and come back to a standing position. Switch legs and repeat, stepping forward with left foot.

> ★ TIP: If your backside's more like a pancake than a nonfat muffin, focus on challenging the muscle by doing more reps or using more weight (but not to the point of injury).

TWISTING LUNGE

In the twisting lunge, you're working in multiple planes of motion and hitting your maximus, medius, and minimus muscles, as well as your obliques (sides of your waist).

1 Stand with feet parallel, holding a light weight in each hand. ◄

2 Take a large step backward with left foot. Turn so upper body now faces to the left, and pivot right foot to the left, so left foot is now facing forward. Lower weights to floor over left leg, being careful to keep left knee in line with left ankle. Pivot back to center, and repeat on opposite leg. ▶

⭐ TIP: I always hear, "It's easy for celebrities to stay motivated." They know their next role often depends on their bodies as well as their craft. Maybe, but your life is your next role. Sometimes it can be hard to keep ourselves psyched up to work out. Your top motivations should be to improve your quality of life (think ability to do whatever life throws at you or you seek out), your health, your kids (so you can be with them longer), your function, and your appearance—in that order.

SIDE LUNGE

The side lunge is great for working the sides of the butt, as well as the inner and outer thighs.

1 Stand with feet together, holding a light weight in each hand. Step wide to the right side with right foot, making sure toes on both feet point straight ahead. ▸

2 Squat and touch weights to floor, one on either side of the right foot. Keep right knee aligned with ankle (you should still be able to see your toes) and back flat. Straighten up and step back to starting position; repeat on left side. ▾

STAGGERED SQUAT

The staggered squat is a great exercise for working the maximus, medius, and also the inner and outer thighs.

1 Stand with feet approximately hip distance apart, toes pointing straight ahead, holding a light weight in each hand with elbows at shoulder level, palms forward. Picture yourself standing in the center of a clock face. Lift right foot and place it between 3 o'clock and 4 o'clock, and place left foot on 12 o'clock. ◄

2 Bend knees, and lower down, as if sitting back into a chair, keeping body weight in heels and being careful not to lean too far forward (you should be able to see your toes past your left knee). As you stand back up, lift right heel slightly. Do all reps on left leg; repeat on opposite side. ▼

★ **TIP: Squeeze it!** Whenever you're doing butt-boosting exercises, focus on squeezing the glutes together with each repetition. This extra contraction will make sure you're homing in on the muscle and working more fibers to their fullest extent.

REVERSE HYPEREXTENSION ON BALL

The reverse hyperextension incorporates a large inflatable stability ball (also known as a Swiss ball, exercise ball, or physioball). You'll exercise your core along with your glutes as you work to stay balanced on the unstable surface of the ball.

1 Lie facedown on a stability ball so belly button and chest are on top of ball. Roll forward slightly, bringing fingertips to floor, keeping most of your weight on ball. Keep feet about 12 to 24 inches apart, slightly turned out, and legs locked. ▸

★ **TIP:** Be sure to work each muscle until it is fully fatigued—that means not being able to do one more rep without losing form. Don't focus too much on the number of reps; instead, concentrate on how your muscles feel. Feel the reps; don't count them.

2 Raise both feet, contracting glutes at top of movement. Hold for 1 count, and lower down (don't touch toes to floor). Repeat. ▸

SINGLE-LEG HIP BRIDGE

You can do the single-leg hip bridge on a stability ball or with one leg on the floor, but it's more of a challenge to use the ball. If you don't have a ball, you can also try using a low chair, ottoman, or sofa. This is a great way to work the maximus muscle, as well as the hamstrings and the inner and outer thighs (adductors and abductors).

1 Lie on floor with sole of right foot on stability ball, knee bent 90 degrees, and left leg extended, perpendicular to floor. Extend arms, with palms down, along sides (harder) or out to sides at shoulder level (easier). ▶

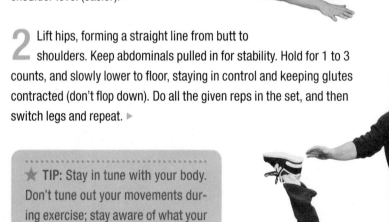

2 Lift hips, forming a straight line from butt to shoulders. Keep abdominals pulled in for stability. Hold for 1 to 3 counts, and slowly lower to floor, staying in control and keeping glutes contracted (don't flop down). Do all the given reps in the set, and then switch legs and repeat. ▶

★ TIP: Stay in tune with your body. Don't tune out your movements during exercise; stay aware of what your muscles are doing to make sure you're achieving correct form and working to your maximum ability.

★ TIP: Get an extra butt-boost when walking: remember to squeeze your glutes together with every step you take. In addition, try to maintain good posture, and allow your arms to swing naturally by your sides. You may feel funny doing it, but you'll feel great afterward.

BUTT BLASTER

The butt blaster mirrors the same movement as the Butt Blaster machine you'll often find at the gym. To make the move a little more challenging, place a light dumbbell in the crease of your leg behind your knee, and use a ball instead of the bench or table.

1 Bending at waist with back straight, lean over a bench or low table with body weight balanced on forearms, palms together (easier), or on a stability ball with arms extended about shoulder distance apart (harder). Keep left knee slightly bent, and bend right knee about 90 degrees, foot flexed.

2 Push sole of right foot toward ceiling, feeling contraction along hamstrings and glutes. Lower and repeat for rest of set, and then switch legs.

★ TIP: Do your workout early in the day. The longer you wait, the greater the chance that you'll be distracted from training at all. If you knock it out first thing, you'll feel better in so many ways all day!

★ TIP: Adding periodic bursts of speed or intensity, otherwise known as interval training, is a great way to burn more calories, improve your overall fitness, and even boost your metabolism for a few more hours after you've finished working out. You can do intervals in almost every form of aerobic exercise, whether you're walking, jogging, running, or using a machine like a stationary cycle, stair climber, or elliptical. Here's how it works: Warm up for a few minutes at a moderate intensity (about a 5 on a scale of 1 to 10). When you're ready, challenge yourself to push your intensity level to about a 7 or 8 for thirty seconds. Then recover at a moderate pace again (5 or 6) for at least ninety seconds. Try to do at least five or six of these intervals in each of your workouts, gradually lengthening your work time and reducing your recovery time until you're working as long as you're resting. (For more on interval training, see Chapter 12.)

THE CARDIO CONNECTION

12

TRAINER: Jeanette Jenkins

WHETHER YOU'RE RUNNING on the treadmill, taking an early-morning power walk, cycling around the park, dancing the night away, or working up a sweat in dozens of other ways, cardiovascular exercise is crucial not only for getting a firm, fit body, but also for living a longer, healthier life. It's the centerpiece of many fitness programs and an essential component of reaching your fitness goals.

Cardio is basically shorthand for any aerobic activity that increases the health and function of the heart, lungs, and circulatory system. There are dozens of well-documented benefits of regular cardiovascular exercise, such as reducing blood pressure and cholesterol levels and improving heart and lung function.

If you're looking to lose weight, aerobic exercise is vital to lowering body fat. The more you train, the better your body is able to call on fat stores for fuel. Your body uses oxygen during aerobic exercise to power the muscles; as you become more aerobically fit, you're able to get more oxygen to the muscles. The more oxygen at the cell site, the more fat you can burn. Simple.

To improve cardiorespiratory fitness and maintain body fat at near-optimal levels, you should aim to do some form of cardio at least three days of the week; the American College of Sports Medicine recommends three to five days a week for most aerobic programs at moderate to high intensity. Studies from the National Weight Control Registry—a database of more than four thousand dieters who have been able to lose thirty or more pounds and maintain that weight loss for at least one year—show that to keep weight off you need to accumulate sixty to ninety minutes of moderate-intensity physical activity each day. (For women, it's an estimated 2,500 calories burned over the course of a week; for men, that number is 3,300 calories.)

But cardio exercises are not all equal. An easy thirty-minute evening stroll is a great way to work off some of your dinner, but it's obviously not as big a calorie burner as doing an hour-long kickboxing class. However, while sprinting works your heart and lungs extra hard, it's unlikely you'll be able to maintain this high-intensity workout for more than a few minutes.

MONITORING YOUR WORKOUT

For getting results, the key is to vary the intensity and length of your cardio exercise. But before you can do that, you need some way to monitor just how hard you are working.

One of the best ways to keep tabs on your intensity level during exercise is with a heart rate monitor, which includes a chest strap that encircles your torso (just under where a bra line would be) to measure your heartbeat and a watch that wirelessly interacts with the device. I recommend that all of my clients use this tool—it's the most accurate way to determine how your body is responding during a workout. If the temperature outside is steaming, you might not be able to work as hard. And if the numbers on the heart rate monitor are high, that's a sign you need to take things down a notch. You can find heart rate monitors on the Web and at most sporting goods or specialty athletic stores. They are available for less than $100, although some of the fancier models that let you upload data to your computer and measure calorie expenditure can run upwards of $300.

A heart rate monitor works by helping you determine the best "zone" in which you should be exercising, based on a percentage of your maximum heart rate. The higher the percentage, the more intense the workout. To estimate your maximum heart rate, subtract your age from 220, and then multiply that number by a percentage to determine your target intensity level. For example, if you are 30 years old, your estimated maximum heart rate is 190 (220 − age 30 = 190). Your target heart rate zone for a moderate level of intensity would be 50 to 60 percent of your max heart rate, or 95 to 114 beats per minute ($190 \times 0.50 = 95$; $190 \times 0.60 = 114$). If you were exercising at a very high intensity of 80 to 90 percent of your max heart rate, your zone would be 152 to 171 beats per minute ($190 \times 0.80 = 152$; $190 \times 0.90 = 171$). If you purchase a heart rate monitor, you'll be able to program these workout zones so you can determine your intensity level at a glance without having to carry numbers in your head. Note that some heart rate monitors use something called the Karvonen formula to determine heart rate zones; this is a more accurate measurement that also takes into account your resting heart rate.

Try it yourself. Use the formula to determine your target heart rate zones during exercise:

1. Subtract your age from 220:

   220 minus my age = _____

2. Multiply the number in step 1 by the following percentages:

   Moderate intensity

   (results from step 1) _____ $\times$ 0.50 = _____
   (results from step 1) _____ $\times$ 0.60 = _____

   Range: _____ to _____ beats per minute

   Moderately hard intensity

   (results from step 1) _____ $\times$ 0.60 = _____
   (results from step 1) _____ $\times$ 0.70 = _____

   Range: _____ to _____ beats per minute

   Challenging intensity

   (results from step 1) _____ $\times$ 0.70 = _____
   (results from step 1) _____ $\times$ 0.80 = _____

   Range: _____ to _____ beats per minute

   Very challenging intensity

   (results from step 1) _____ $\times$ 0.80 = _____
   (results from step 1) _____ $\times$ 0.90 = _____

   Range: _____ to _____ beats per minute

   Extremely challenging intensity

   (results from step 1) _____ $\times$ 0.90 = _____
   (results from step 1) _____ $\times$ 0.99 = _____

   Range: _____ to _____ beats per minute

WHERE DO I FIT IN?

To quickly estimate where your target heart rate zone should be during basic aerobic activity (50 to 75 percent of your maximum heart rate), find the category that comes closest to your age in the following chart.

Age	Target Heart Rate Zone 50%–75%	Average Maximum Heart Rate 100%
20–30	98–146 beats per minute	195
31–40	93–138 beats per minute	185
41–50	88–131 beats per minute	175
51–60	83–123 beats per minute	165
61+	78–116 beats per minute	155

MORE WAYS TO MONITOR

In addition to using a heart rate monitor, you can keep tabs on your workout intensity in a few other ways:

◉ **Manual heart rate:** It's not as accurate as a heart rate monitor, but you can compute your target heart rate zone manually by taking your pulse either on your wrist or neck for ten seconds, then multiplying by 6 to determine your heart rate for one minute. Plug that number into the preceding chart to determine your training zones.

> ★ TIP: It's a good idea to have a physical before you begin any exercise program. Know your blood pressure, cholesterol numbers, and other important measures. If your weight stays the same but your cholesterol levels go down, that is still something to feel good about.

◉ **Rate of perceived exertion:** Since most of us are unlikely to work out with a calculator and it's difficult to do math while working up a sweat, exercise physiologists also recommend following your rate of perceived exertion (RPE). Basically, it's a scale of how hard you perceive your intensity to be on a scale of 1 to 10, with 1 being the easiest and 10 the most difficult.

TARGET TRAINING ZONES

HEART RATE ZONE	RATE OF PERCEIVED EXERTION	TALK TEST
< 30%	1–2 (very light)	Able to speak easily
30%–49%	3–4 (moderate)	Speak with some effort
50%–74%	5–6 (somewhat strong)	Speak mostly in phrases, effort
75%–84%	7–8 (very strong)	Speak mostly in words, effort
85%+	9–10 (maximal effort)	Unable to speak

○ **Talk test:** A third option is to use something called the talk test to gauge your intensity level. I like to recommend using this method in conjunction with RPEs to more easily determine how hard my clients are working. At a moderate level like a neighborhood stroll, it's easy to have a conversation with a friend as you walk. But as anyone who's had to sprint to catch a bus or run up a flight of stairs knows, at very high intensity levels, it's difficult to get out even short answers, if you can speak at all.

When you're following the programs recommended in this chapter, either use a heart rate monitor or use a combination of RPEs and the talk test to determine your target training zones.

ESTABLISHING YOUR CARDIO PLAN

When I work with Queen Latifah and other clients, we do a mix of several types of aerobic workouts over the course of a week. One day we might do a longer, slower steady-state program that has her working at a moderate intensity for up to an hour—for example, going on a gradual hike where the incline gets steeper as we progress. Other times we'll do intervals of walking up a steep hill or walking flat and jogging on the treadmill. Often we'll combine our strength and cardio into one big total body workout that sculpts her arms, legs, abs, and butt while also elevating her heart rate.

Your weekly workout plan should also include a mix of cardio activities. Combining intervals one day and a moderately paced longer workout the next will challenge your heart and lungs and blast fat while reducing your risk of injury or burnout. It doesn't really matter what type of exercise you choose to do—only that you do it. The key to consistency, though, is to find a workout you enjoy. So if you're a walker, make walking the key part of your routine, either outside or on the treadmill. If you'd rather use a machine at the gym like the elliptical trainer or stair climber, go with that. If you enjoy cycling, either get outside or hop on a stationary bike. Or think outside traditional cardio activities, and try something totally new: take a dance class, sign up for swimming lessons, or head outside for the trails or ski slopes.

The next step is to put together a program based on your goals. The A-List Workout has several goals, all of which include some measure of cardio exercises at least three days a week. Use the chart on the next page to determine how to work these cardio routines into your A-List Workout goals.

PLAN DETAILS

Now that you've seen the schedule, here's exactly what you'll need to be doing for your workout plan.

Beginners

I can't stress highly enough that if you're either new to fitness or just coming back after a long layoff, you need to start slowly and build gradually. Ideally, you should get a physical exam from your doctor, so you know where you are starting out. Don't rely solely on the scale for measuring your progress. Measure your body fat; the inches around your hips, thighs, abs, and arms; cholesterol levels; and blood pressure. Knowing these numbers will give you a starting point from which to improve your health and fitness.

★ TIP: If you are just starting out, start slowly and build gradually. Begin with my aerobic base training routine to stay motivated. This way you won't burn out when it comes time to do the more challenging workouts.

If you fall into the beginner category, congratulations! You're about to take a very important step toward achieving better health and appearance. But don't take on too much too soon. I know many newcomers to exercise who are diligent about spending an hour on the treadmill every day. That lasts about a week before burnout sets in. Instead, I would rather see you set the following

YOUR A-LIST CARDIO ROUTINE

◎ **Beginner program:** Do 2 to 3 aerobic base workouts per week for the first 4 to 6 weeks. For the next 4 to 8 weeks, add 1 interval workout to your program.

◎ **Total body tone-up:** Do 3 to 4 cardio workouts a week, including at least 2 steady-state and 1 or 2 interval workouts (add an optional circuit routine).

◎ **Target trouble zones:** Do 4 to 5 cardio workouts a week, including at least 2 steady-state and 1 interval workouts, along with 1 circuit workout.

◎ **Weight loss workout:** Do 5 to 6 cardio workouts a week, including at least 2 steady-state, 2 interval, and 1 circuit workouts.

goal: practice aerobic base training three to six times a week for twenty to forty-five minutes at an intensity level of 50 to 75 percent of your max heart rate. That translates to an RPE of 5 to 6, where you are able to speak but mostly in phrases; talking requires some effort.

You can follow any activity of your choosing that elevates your heart rate to the desired level. Just do something you enjoy, whether that's walking, swimming, riding a bike, taking a dance class, or using a machine at the gym. Continue to do this for four to six weeks, until you build up a base—or until you can comfortably get through a thirty-minute workout without feeling fatigued.

After the first four to six weeks, you will have built up a good aerobic base. You can also begin doing the interval workouts in this chapter; follow the beginner's column. Note that you should still follow the beginner recommendations on the strength routine.

Intermediate to Advanced

If you have been exercising regularly for some time and have already built up a solid aerobic base, you can take your routine to the next level by incorporating several types of cardiovascular workouts. I recommend doing a mix of the following:

● **Steady-state workouts:** Basically, a steady-state workout is just a continuation of the beginner aerobic base workout. The idea is to do some form of aerobic exercise at a moderate to somewhat high intensity (50 to 75 percent of your max heart rate; RPE 5 to 6; you can speak mostly in short sentences or phrases but with a little bit of effort) for forty-five to sixty minutes. This type of continuous training helps you continue to maintain an aerobic base and burn excess body fat.

● **Interval workouts:** Add some interval routines into your weekly plan. According to dozens of studies, interval workouts—periodic bursts of intensity followed by moderate recovery periods—are one of the best ways to improve endurance, burn more calories in a shorter time period, and even temporarily bump up your metabolic rate after exercise, also known as the afterburn effect.

There are many types of interval workouts, based on varying the intensity of the work interval (speed or resistance) or the duration of the work interval (distance or time) as well as the duration of rest or recovery and the number of times you repeat the interval. My favorite interval workout is described in the sidebar on the next page. It uses progressively longer work periods to challenge you both physically and mentally. However, you can also mix up the length of the intervals, the intensity, the number, and the amount of recovery time for variety and as a way to stay motivated. If your goal is weight loss, do two of these high-intensity interval workouts each week.

> ★ TIP: Write your workouts into your calendar, and then put it on the fridge so you know exactly what you have to do that week. This will serve as a reminder for your weekly goals and help you stay on track.

● **Circuit workouts:** When you're pressed for time, it is possible to get in a total body workout *and* a cardio routine simultaneously. The key: circuit workouts that help you sculpt strong, sexy muscles while also keeping your heart rate elevated. I've designed two circuit routines: one uses just your body weight for a major burn that you can do anywhere, and the other uses dumbbells for additional resistance and toning benefits. Don't rest for more than a few seconds between each exercise unless absolutely necessary. Also, don't do the circuit workout with weights on the day following any strength routine, and avoid doing two circuit workouts two days in a row. Repeat either circuit three times total. Do the exercises back to back with no rest, but then take a ninety-second break between each full circuit to recover. You'll burn an estimated 325 to 450 calories in thirty minutes.

▶ MY FAVORITE INTERVAL WORKOUT

You can do this workout on any cardio machine at the gym or by walking or running outside. Use the given heart rate zone or RPE to determine your effort level. If you're on a cardio machine, use the display timer to monitor when your pace and intensity need to change; if you're outside, use a heart rate monitor or a digital watch.

| | | HEART RATE | | |
| | | | INTERMEDIATE/ | |
MINUTES	PACE	BEGINNER	ADVANCED	RPE
0:00–5:00	Warm up	60%–70%	60%–70%	5
5:00–7:00	Begin to intensify	65%–75%	70%–80%	6, 7
7:00–11:00	Maintain steady pace	70%–75%	75%–80%	7
11:00–12:00	Sprint, 1 min.	80%–90%	85%–95%	8, 9
12:00–14:00	Recover, lower intensity	65%–75%	75%	6, 7
14:00–15:30	Sprint, 90 sec.	80%–90%	85%–95%	8, 9
15:30–17:30	Recover, lower intensity	65%–75%	75%	6, 7
17:30–19:15	Sprint, 1 min. 45 sec.	80%–90%	85%–95%	8, 9
19:15–21:15	Recover, lower intensity	65%–75%	75%	6, 7
21:15–23:15	Sprint, 2 min.	80%–90%	85%–95%	8, 9
23:15–25:30	Recover, lower intensity	65%–75%	75%	6, 7
25:30–30:30	Gradual acceleration	75%–90%	75%–95%	8, 9
	(Increase speed by 10% each minute.)			
30:30–35:00	Cool down	60%–65%	60%–65%	5

THE CARDIO WORKOUT

CIRCUIT 1: NO WEIGHTS

The first routine is a great do-anywhere cardio/strength circuit that uses just your body weight for resistance. Repeat the entire circuit three times.

1 PUSH-UP: Do these on knees (easier) or toes (harder). Do 15 to 25 reps. ▶

2 REPEATER KNEE: Bring left knee toward right shoulder, diagonally crossing your torso. Repeat left knee for 25 reps, and then repeat same movement with right leg. Do 25 reps. ▼

3 FRONT KICK: Kick directly in front of body at about waist height, and then step back with opposite leg and touch floor. Do all of the reps on one leg, and then repeat on the other leg. Do 25 reps. ▶

> ★ **TIP:** Splurge on a new workout outfit, such as new sneakers, a top, shorts, or some other form of workout clothes. A nice outfit can make a big difference in keeping you motivated, and you can look forward to showing off your new body while you exercise!

4 ISOMETRIC BALANCING STICK/BACK FLY: Stand balancing on right leg, muscles firm and eyes focused forward. Slowly lift left leg behind you as you bring torso parallel to floor. From this position, slowly pull both arms back like wings, squeezing shoulder blades together. Do 15 reps total; switch sides and repeat. ▼

5 BALANCING LEG ABDUCTION: Stand balancing on left leg, both arms reaching above head. Slowly lift right leg out to side, keeping hips square to front. Do 25 reps; lower leg, and repeat on opposite side. ▶

6 JOG IN PLACE, PUNCHING FORWARD WITH ALTERNATING HANDS: Do 100 punches total. ▶▶

7 **LATERAL SIDE SHUFFLE:** Stand in squat position with knees slightly bent, arms in front at waist height. Step right foot to right side, and then bring left foot to right side, stepping laterally. Touch floor with right hand. Return to squat and step to left side, first with left foot and then with right. Touch floor with left hand. Repeat step/touch combo, moving as quickly as possible, for a total of 10 to 15 reps to each side. ◄

8 **STATIONARY LUNGE WITH ROTATION:** Stand with left foot 3 to 4 feet in front of right, toes pointing forward, arms lifted to shoulder height, palms down. Bend left knee 90 degrees, keeping left knee aligned over left ankle; drop right knee toward floor as deeply as possible without touching floor. Holding this position, rotate torso and shoulders to left side; hold 1 count, and return to center. Do 15 to 20 reps; switch legs, and repeat, rotating this time to the right. ►

★ **TIP:** Set realistic goals. It's really important to have specific goals—not just "I want to lose weight," but to lose ten pounds by a certain date. It's also important to focus on your health, not just the numbers on a scale. Exercise is not just about making you look better in front of a mirror. You'll stay hooked on working out consistently if you feel better, too.

9 AB CIRCUIT: Do 25 reps of each of the following abdominal exercises.

Crunch: Lie on floor faceup with hands behind head. Lift shoulders and upper back off the floor, curling up by engaging your abdominals. Keep head in hands, and chin about fist distance from chest. ▸

Bicycle crunch: Lie on floor faceup with knees into chest, hands behind head. Extend right leg 45 degrees from floor; bring right shoulder toward left knee. Reverse the move, bringing left shoulder toward right knee. ▸

Reverse crunch: Lie on floor faceup with knees bent and pulled toward chest, arms at sides with palms on floor. Using lower abs, slowly lift tailbone and lower back off the floor. Be careful not to swing legs or use too much momentum; the momentum should come from your abs. ▸

10 DOUBLE LEG EXTENSION: Lie on floor faceup with hands behind head. Stack knees over hips, and pull navel to spine, engaging lower abdominal fibers; keep hands behind head. Make sure lower back stays in contact with floor. Exhale as you extend legs out in front of you about 45 degrees, squeezing abs tight while lifting head and shoulders off floor, and hold for 3 to 5 seconds. Bring knees back in over hips, and repeat for 8 to 10 reps. ▾

CIRCUIT 2: WEIGHTS

Do this circuit if you have access to light dumbbells and want to increase your intensity level. Repeat the entire circuit three times. Use two- to eight-pound dumbbells where indicated.

1 PUSH-UP/PLANK COMBO: Do 10 push-ups, on either knees (beginner) or toes (intermediate to advanced). After the 10th rep, hold body in the up position (plank pose) for 30 to 60 seconds. End with 10 more push-ups. (Top three photos.) ▸

2 REVERSE LUNGE/KICK WITH BICEPS CURL: Hold one weight in each hand with arms at sides, palms up.

Step back into lunge position with left leg, bending right knee 90 degrees and keeping knee aligned with ankle; at the same time, curl weights toward shoulders. ▾

As you rise up, kick forward with left leg while lowering weights toward thighs. Repeat. Do 15 to 25 reps on this leg. ▸▸

3 **REVERSE LUNGE/KICK WITH FRONT RAISE:** Hold weights in both hands, palms facing body.

Step back into lunge position with right leg, bending left knee 90 degrees and lifting arms to shoulder height, palms down. ◄

As you rise up, kick forward with right leg while lowering arms to sides; repeat. Do 15 to 25 reps on this leg. ►

4 **BALANCING LEG ABDUCTION:** Stand, balancing on left leg, arms extended above head and holding weights with palms forward. Slowly lift right leg out to side, keeping hips square to front. Do 25 reps; lower leg and repeat on opposite side. ▼

5 **LATERAL SIDE SHUFFLE:** Stand in semi-squat position with knees slightly bent, arms in front at waist height. Step right foot to right side, and then bring left foot to right, stepping laterally. Touch floor with right hand, and then repeat, stepping to left with left foot first, then right. Touch floor with left hand. Repeat step/touch combo, moving as quickly as possible, for a total of 10 to 15 reps to each side. For an additional challenge, hold weights throughout. ►

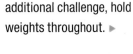

6 SQUAT WITH SHOULDER PRESS: Stand with weights at shoulder height, elbows bent with palms facing forward.

Squat, bending knees 90 degrees and keeping weight in heels. Don't let knees move past toes. ▶

Stand up, straightening arms and extending weights overhead. Lower and repeat for 10 reps. ▶▶

7 SQUAT WITH SHOULDER PRESS PLUS ROTATION: Stand with feet parallel or turned out to corners. Hold weights at shoulder height, with elbows bent and palms facing forward.

Squat, bending knees 90 degrees and keeping knees aligned over toes. Keep weights at shoulder height. ▼

Stand up, rotating torso to left and extending right arm toward ceiling. Return to start, and repeat 10 times. ▼

Repeat in the other direction, rotating torso to right side and extending left arm toward ceiling. Do 10 reps total.

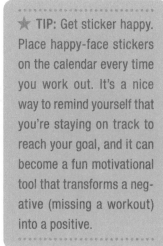

★ TIP: Get sticker happy. Place happy-face stickers on the calendar every time you work out. It's a nice way to remind yourself that you're staying on track to reach your goal, and it can become a fun motivational tool that transforms a negative (missing a workout) into a positive.

8 BACK ROW: Stand with feet hip distance apart and knees bent.

Hold weights at sides with palms facing in. Lean forward from waist, keeping abdominals firm and head aligned with spine. ▶

Pull elbows back, keeping arms close to sides and bringing weights next to ribs. Hold 1 count; lower and repeat. Do 15 to 25 reps total. ▶ ▶

9 Jog in place, punching forward at chin level. (Use very light weights if you are using dumbbells.) Do 25 punches with each arm. Don't lock elbows as you punch; maintain control as you punch toward the same spot. ◀

⏮ *M*USIC MATTERS

Listen to music while you exercise. It's a huge motivator. One recent study found that exercisers who worked out to their own music lasted approximately ten minutes longer; had lower heart rates, oxygen consumption, and blood pressure levels; and burned an average of 77.5 more calories than those who went sans music. I offer my clients different playlists when they are working out: it makes a big difference for putting 100 percent into your workout.

10 **PUSH KICK:** Stand with feet hip distance apart, weights together in front of chest.

Turn right foot out, and tap toes to floor, shifting weight to right leg. ◄

Pull left knee in toward chest, and kick out to side, leading with the heel and keeping left inner thigh parallel to floor. Retract heel, and lower leg; repeat. Do 25 reps; switch legs. ▼

11 **AB CIRCUIT:** Do 25 reps of each of the following abdominal exercises:

Crunch: Lie on floor faceup with hands behind head. Lift shoulders and upper back off the floor, curling up by engaging abdominals. Keep head in hands and chin about fist distance from chest. ▼

★ **TIP:** Don't just look at the numbers on a scale as measures of your success. Changes in body fat are equally, if not more, important; you'll want to be building lean, sexy muscle and dropping the fat. If your pants feel looser or you've dropped a dress size, that's a great way to see that your program is on track.

Bicycle crunch: Lie on floor faceup with knees into chest, hands behind head. Extend left leg 4 to 6 inches from floor, then reverse; bring right shoulder toward left knee. Repeat, bringing left shoulder toward right knee. ▼

Reverse crunch: Lie on floor faceup with knees bent and pulled toward chest, arms at sides with palms on floor. Using lower abs, slowly lift tailbone and lower back off the floor. ▲

12 **DOUBLE LEG EXTENSION:** Lie on floor faceup with hands behind head. Stack knees over hips, and pull navel to spine, engaging lower abdominal fibers; keep hands behind head. Make sure lower back stays in contact with the floor. Exhale and extend legs out in front of you, about 45 degrees while lifting head and shoulders off floor. Squeeze abs tight, and hold for 3 to 5 seconds. Bring knees back in over hips, and repeat for 8 to 10 reps. ▶

> ★ **TIP:** If weight loss is your goal, choose aerobic exercise where you need to support your own body weight in order to burn more calories, such as walking, jogging, or using the stair climber or elliptical. By doing as much weight-bearing activity as you can, you will maximize your cardio burn.

GETTING FLEXIBLE

GETTING
FLEXIBLE

TRAINER: Ashley Borden

FLEXIBILITY TRAINING is an important part of maintaining a fit, healthy body and something that I emphasize with all of my clients. Over the years, I have worked with several prominent actresses, musicians, and entertainment executives to help them get strong, fit, and flexible.

I teach something called the L.I.S.T. (List Integrated Systematic Training) system, a program that was developed by Karl List and combines elements from yoga, Pilates, and the fundamental principles of biomechanics. The training emphasizes proprioceptive work (an awareness of where and how your body moves), balance training, core strength, and flexibility. I was introduced to Karl several years ago after an injury that had pulled every muscle in my upper back. He took me through a L.I.S.T. rehabilitation program, which helped me relearn how to fire my muscles properly and strengthen muscles I didn't even know I had, resulting in a body that I never knew I could achieve. Armed with this knowledge, I began to integrate this system with my own clients and witnessed unbelievable improvement in their flexibility and core strength.

This method of flexibility training is not the type of old-school stretching you may have done back in gym class, where you held one static stretch for thirty seconds. Instead, it's based on a technique called active-isolated stretching, which involves contracting one muscle group while stretching the opposite. Since most muscles work in pairs (think quadriceps and hamstrings or biceps and triceps), the idea is that when you contract or shorten one group, the opposite muscle will relax and lengthen, thus allowing a deeper stretch. For example, when you contract your biceps, you stretch your triceps. To stretch your hamstrings, you contract your quads. Stay with me; this will make more sense as we move on!

Yoga has drawn millions of devoted participants (especially among the celebrity set), and one of its many benefits is flexibility. However, the challenge with yoga is that the focus is not on the end point of contraction. Whereas in yoga the focus is just on the stretch, the L.I.S.T. system focuses on the contraction *and* the stretch. This gives you a deeper, more controlled stretch and more definition of the contracting muscle while discouraging injury.

An invaluable part of stretching is breathing correctly. Breathing itself is, quite obviously, second nature. But I teach my clients to practice "belly breathing": Think about expanding your waistline outward as you inhale deeply through your nose. Then, on a count of eight, exhale the air out of your lungs through your mouth. You'll see your belly rise and fall with each breath. The deeper you breathe, the more oxygen you'll bring into your muscles, which is crucial to getting the most out of your stretching. It also helps combat stress and anxiety.

One more important note about stretching: it not only reduces your risk of injury (which many people think of as the foremost benefit), it also spills over into other areas of your workout. If one muscle group, such as your quads, is tight, that will prevent others, like your glutes, from firing correctly. That can lead to compromised performance during cardiovascular activities like running, and diminished strength-training results. Flexible muscles also contribute to better posture, which can help you look longer and leaner.

⟩ *S*TRETCH FUNDAMENTALS

When you stretch, muscle fibers send a signal to the spine, which sets off the stretch reflex. This reflex is a protective mechanism that actually attempts to resist change in muscle length by causing stretched muscles to contract. It's one reason that static stretching can feel painful at times, especially if you're not flexible to begin with; it's also important not to overstretch the muscles.

The exercises on these pages are designed to increase your range of motion in some of our biggest problem areas, especially for people who are sedentary or who work at a desk many hours a day. I call it "computer body," when you're constantly hunched over the desk, the phone tucked under one ear, legs crossed and typing an e-mail. Soon the muscles in your neck, back, hamstrings,

STRETCHING: THE TRUTH

There are many different forms of stretching, and they are not all created equal. Here's a look at some of the most popular ways to limber up:

◉ **Ballistic stretching** uses momentum in an attempt to force your limbs or joints beyond their normal range of motion. A common example is reaching down to touch your toes and then bouncing in place to go deeper. This method does not generally increase flexibility and, in fact, can lead to injury because it does not allow your muscles to relax in the stretched position.

◉ **Dynamic stretching,** often done right before a workout, usually imitates specific movements from the sport or activity in an exaggerated but controlled way. Examples are making large arm circles before a tennis match or jogging in place and bringing your knees to your chest before a running race.

◉ **Static stretching,** probably the most widely used technique, is where you passively stretch a muscle to the point of mild discomfort by holding it in a stretched state for an extended period, anywhere from ten seconds to one minute.

◉ **PNF,** or proprioceptive neuromuscular facilitation, is a two-person technique, which means you'll need a partner (or trainer) to assist you. It involves your partner actively stretching you with a combination of altering contraction and relaxation of both the target muscle and its opposing muscle, such as quadriceps and the hamstrings. There's usually a push phase surrounded by a relaxation phase, repeated several times.

◉ **Active-isolated stretching** works with both the target muscle (e.g., the hamstrings) and its opposing muscle group (in this case, the quads). It works on the theory that the stretch reflex, the body's natural defense mechanism that stops it from overstretching, can be overcome by lengthening muscle in its relaxed state. That means you'll contract the agonist, or opposite, muscle while stretching the antagonist, or target muscle.

and chest all become tight and less functional. The following exercises can change all that.

THE GETTING FLEXIBLE WORKOUT

HAMSTRING STRETCH SERIES

The following hamstring stretch series is a great way to stretch the hamstrings, an area that is chronically tight for most women and men. Do the series straight through, and then switch sides at the end. For an advanced variation, do this move standing; you'll work your glutes to maintain your balance, while also improving your balance skills.

1 Place a small folded towel behind head and lie on the floor faceup with legs extended. Lift right leg, interlacing fingers behind hamstrings, as close to your groin as comfortable; focus eyes on chest, and keep chin down, jaw pulled in. Tighten pelvic floor. As you slightly pull hamstring toward chest, contract right quads, and simultaneously flex right foot, pushing heel toward wall in front of you. Relax and repeat; do 5 reps total on right leg.

★ TIP: Change your breathing. Don't always breathe the same way. Bring new awareness to your workout by sometimes inhaling on exertion and exhaling on release; then switch and do exhaling on exertion and inhaling on release.

2 Repeat, this time turning right thigh slightly outward, so heel points in; do 5 reps. ▶

3 Relax and repeat, this time turning right thigh slightly inward so heel points out and toes point in; do 5 reps. Switch legs and repeat series on left side. ▶▶

MODIFIED PIGEON

The modified pigeon, a slight variation on a yoga exercise, really stretches the piriformis, a deep muscle in your glute that is often short and tight, especially for those who sit a lot during the day.

1 Begin on floor in a full push-up position, palms aligned under shoulders. ▶

2 Place right knee on floor near right shoulder, with right heel by left hip. Lower left knee to floor. Keep body weight on forearms, with palms flat, eyes looking down. (If you're more flexible, bring chest down to floor and extend arms in front of you.) Pull navel in toward spine, and tighten muscles of pelvic floor. Contract left glute. ▶

3 To deepen stretch, lift left leg, and curl toes under while pressing ball of left foot into the floor, pushing through heel. Bend knee to floor, and release. Do 5 reps total; then switch sides and repeat.

COBRA

Stretching your abdominal muscles is just as important as strengthening them. Stretching the abdominals helps keep the chest lifted, resulting in better posture. This exercise helps strengthen your deep abs while stretching the rectus abdominis, or "six-pack" muscle.

1 Lie facedown on floor with thumbs directly under shoulders and fingers spread wide. Keep legs extended with tops of feet on the floor; tuck hips into the floor, and squeeze glutes while tightening pelvic floor. ▶

2 Pushing down through each thumb and index finger, lift chest toward wall in front of you. Visualize pulling palms toward you as you bring chest forward. Keep shoulders away from ears. Relax and repeat; do 5 reps total. ◀

C-CURVE

I love the C-curve for stretching the lower-back muscles, which are often both weak and tight. You'll also feel the stretch in the back of the hamstrings and along the back of your neck.

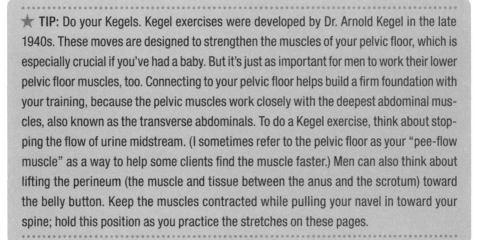

1 Sit on floor with knees bent, heels on floor about 1 foot in front of glutes. Interlace fingers behind both hamstrings, keeping elbows pointing out to sides. Round spine forward, tightening pelvic floor and pulling navel in toward spine; keep eyes gazing at belly button. Inhale through nose, and exhale, drawing navel in even tighter. ▸

2 Extend left leg, pushing left heel toward ceiling while pulling pinkie toe back. At the same time, push down with right foot into the floor. Bend forward while extending leg. Do 5 reps; then switch sides and repeat. ▸

> ★ **TIP:** Do your Kegels. Kegel exercises were developed by Dr. Arnold Kegel in the late 1940s. These moves are designed to strengthen the muscles of your pelvic floor, which is especially crucial if you've had a baby. But it's just as important for men to work their lower pelvic floor muscles, too. Connecting to your pelvic floor helps build a firm foundation with your training, because the pelvic muscles work closely with the deepest abdominal muscles, also known as the transverse abdominals. To do a Kegel exercise, think about stopping the flow of urine midstream. (I sometimes refer to the pelvic floor as your "pee-flow muscle" as a way to help some clients find the muscle faster.) Men can also think about lifting the perineum (the muscle and tissue between the anus and the scrotum) toward the belly button. Keep the muscles contracted while pulling your navel in toward your spine; hold this position as you practice the stretches on these pages.

ONE-ARM REACH

The one-arm reach is an active stretch, because you are using your body weight for added resistance to enhance the exercise while really stretching out your shoulders. Be sure your neck is not being crammed as you rest your forehead on the floor. Your shoulders, not your neck, should be taking most of the weight.

1 Kneel on all fours with wrists aligned under shoulders and knees under hips. Curl toes under so balls of both feet are pushing into the floor.

2 Bring forehead to the floor, and slide the pinkie side edge of your right hand along the floor in front of you. (Keep left palm flat on floor with left elbow close to side.) Press shoulders back and down while pushing down through balls of feet and tightening glutes. Return to start by pushing down on left palm and sliding right hand back toward shoulders. Do 5 reps; switch sides and repeat.

★ **TIP:** Don't let your shoulders hug your ears. Many people walk around with their shoulders hunched up and their back tight. Lift your shoulders up, and then press them all the way down as you exhale. Practice doing this move throughout the day, not just when you're working out.

SPLIT SQUAT

You'll work both your hip flexors and your quads with the split squat. It's a great move for runners and cyclists, who are chronically tight in these areas, as well as for anyone who sits at a job all day and suffers from a flabby tush. To make it even more challenging, put one foot on a folded yoga mat or balance disc.

1 Stand with feet hip distance apart. Step right foot out about one stride's length in front of left. Keep weight balanced over both feet, and spread toes. Interlace fingers, placing hands under ribs; pull shoulders down away from ears. Tighten muscles of pelvic floor, and squeeze left glutes; tuck pelvis under, bending left knee and coming onto toes of left foot. ▶

2 Slowly bend both knees about 90 degrees, coming down in 3 counts; keep weight equal on both feet. Rise back to start, coming back up in 3 counts. Do 5 reps; switch legs and repeat. ◀

ROLL WITH IT

Foam rollers are a fabulous tool for strengthening the core (see Chapter 4), but I also really like them as a way to improve flexibility. They are one of the best stretching/massage devices out there. They're key to preventing injury, as well as help speed recovery after a workout. All of my clients roll out before they begin their sessions with me.

Rolling a tight muscle along the top of the foam roller helps break up scar tissue that can be formed along muscle fibers. It's called myofascial release, and it's a great way to reduce these adhesions, or what some people refer to as knots. Your flexibility and range of motion will increase, and you'll lower your risk of injury and improve circulation to whatever area you're targeting, thus increasing your metabolic rate. It's actually the cheapest massage you'll find. If you don't have access to a foam roller, you can use a weighted ball, such as a six-inch medicine ball, or try taping two tennis balls together. Lie on top of the roller or ball, and slowly roll back and forth for one to two minutes. If you reach a painful spot, stop, pull your belly in and hold, moving just a few inches in either direction for thirty to forty seconds. Key areas to target include the quads, iliotibial band (outer thigh to inner knee), piriformis (deep gluteals), calves, hamstrings, and upper back.

ROLL-UP

The perfect way to end this stretch sequence, the roll-up draws everything together to stretch both the front and back of your body while calming your nervous system.

1 Lie on the floor faceup, with knees bent and feet flat on floor, arms at sides with palms up. Inhale, then exhale, tightening pelvic floor and drawing navel in toward spine.

2 Keeping pelvic muscles tight, squeeze glutes, and then slowly lift hips as you roll back off the floor one vertebra at a time. Be sure to keep squeezing glutes as you roll up and push through heels. When you're all the way up, inhale again. Exhale, squeezing glutes; then roll slowly back down to the floor one vertebra at a time.

LARRY KRUG ★ THE·A-LIST·DIET

14

THE A-LIST DIET

TRAINER: █ Larry Krug █

SOMETIMES MY CLIENTS ask me which is more important when you're trying to lose weight: a healthy diet or a comprehensive exercise plan. I've always thought that it's an equal partnership, fifty-fifty. The two work hand in hand.

Losing weight isn't easy, even for celebrities. Unfortunately, in Hollywood, there are endless supposed "miracle diets" that promise to help you drop pounds in a flash. Over the years, I've seen countless claims on easy ways to shed the fat—everything from the wacky (juice fasts, cabbage soup, or the grapefruit diet) to the downright dangerous (prescription drugs and some shady herbal supplements).

But at the end of the day, the only thing that is going to help you lose weight (and keep it off) is to follow a simple formula: calories out must be greater than calories in. In other words, you must expend more calories than you consume, plain and simple. That doesn't mean starving yourself or

> ★ **TIP:** Make time for tea. If you're still feeling hungry after a meal, try drinking some green tea. Besides being rich in antioxidants, green tea may help reduce hunger pains by relaxing the muscles of the stomach lining.

eating small quantities of unhealthful foods: any deprivation or very low calorie diet will result in weight loss, but as soon as you begin eating normally again, the pounds will bounce back. Your long-term success is based on long-term healthy eating.

WHAT TO EAT?

So what does it take to eat healthfully? A successful diet plan doesn't just mean skipping the side of fries or shunning dessert after dinner. To really see results, you need to change the way you think about eating entirely.

If your goal is to lose weight, you need to watch the amount of carbohydrates you consume. I'm not advocating a crazy low-carb diet. After all, with the intensity required for most of the A-List Workout, you'll need an adequate amount of carbs to fuel your muscles. Carbohydrates are the body's first and preferred source of energy. But I generally tell my clients who are looking to jump-start their weight loss that about 45 percent of their diet should be made up mostly of "healthy" carbs (see graph). That means you need to eat more of your carbs in the form of fruits, vegetables, and whole grains and very little "junk" carbs, such as white flour, white rice, pasta, and of course, cookies, candy, soda, and the like. About 35 percent of your daily calorie intake should be based on good sources of protein: lean meats, fish, poultry, and egg whites. Finally, the remaining 20 percent of your daily calories should come from healthy fats like olive oils, certain vegetables, and other nonanimal choices. Fats may sound like the enemy, but they are required for many important bodily functions, from protecting the nerves to making your skin look healthy.

One reason I break my meal plan into this ratio (45 percent carbs, 35 percent protein, and 20 percent fat) is that I believe it's the optimum way to keep your body fired up for your exercise plan and give it enough fuel to fully recover after each workout. Although this amount of protein is not as high as in some other diets, in my experience it's an adequate amount to suit your needs. When you're exercising, espe-

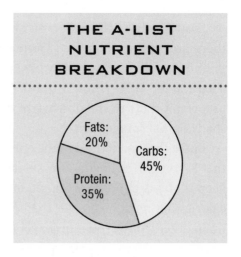

THE A-LIST NUTRIENT BREAKDOWN

Fats: 20%

Carbs: 45%

Protein: 35%

cially as intensely as on the A-List Workout, your body breaks down protein stores. Your body needs more protein to help rebuild the muscles and improve its strength. Note that protein is also an important part of appetite control (you're less likely to want to start snacking if you have a little bit of protein with each meal), and it's also an essential part of keeping your metabolism revved up throughout the day, because your body expends energy simply to break down and digest protein. In addition, protein helps balance your blood sugar by counterbalancing insulin levels in the bloodstream.

THE GIST OF THE GLYCEMIC INDEX

One other important consideration when you're following a healthful diet is to determine where your food choices fall in the glycemic index (GI). The GI is an index of how fast sugars appear in the bloodstream. It ranges from 0 to 100. The higher the number, the faster the food gets into your bloodstream.

That's important when you're trying to lose weight, because the rate at which carbohydrates enter your bloodstream can make a big difference in what your body chooses to store as fat and what it uses for fuel. A food with a high GI—a slice of white bread, for example—enters the system so quickly that it cannot be broken down fast enough, so the body simply diverts the carbohydrates to the fat stores to be broken down later and stored as fat. In contrast, a lower-GI food—oatmeal, for example—will enter the bloodstream slowly. That allows your body enough time to break down the carbohydrates without having them stored as fat.

The bottom-line message here is this: in general, to lose weight, you're better off sticking with lower-GI foods. In addition to their role in fat storage and fuel, most lower-GI foods (especially complex carbohydrates like whole wheat or whole grains) are high in fiber, so they'll also help keep you feeling more full for a longer period of time, which means you'll be less likely to snack between meals.

INSULIN'S ROLE IN CURBING CRAVINGS

There's another important reason to make sure you're eating a diet that's balanced in the different primary nutrients. When you eat carbohydrates, your pancreas releases the hormone insulin into your bloodstream. Insulin's primary function is to transport blood sugar from the blood to your muscles and liver, where the excess carbs (now called glycogen) are stored. When insulin is released, carbohydrates become the body's primary source of energy. High levels of insulin may cause carbohydrates to be stored as fat, which stops your body from burning its fat stores.

Therefore, it's important to regulate the amount of insulin released into the bloodstream. By controlling your insulin levels, your body will use more stored fat as an energy source. The key is to make sure you eat foods that stabilize your blood sugar (and thus your insulin levels). Too much insulin will cause blood sugar levels to drop. And when your blood sugar falls too low, it stimulates your appetite to eat more sugar, which in turn produces more insulin. When you get caught in this cycle, the only way you can get your blood sugar levels up again is to eat more sugar (or more refined carbs that cause high sugar production).

So how do you break this carbohydrate cycle? By eating the right amount of fat and protein in your daily diet and the right amount of unrefined or low-glycemic carbohydrates, which will keep your blood sugar levels balanced. With the correct combination, you can regulate the body's insulin levels and radically reduce your cravings.

YOUR A-LIST WORKOUT FOODS

What does all this mean when it's time to take a trip to the grocery store? I've given you lists of some of my favorite food choices that are healthful sources of carbohydrates, protein, and fat. Each serving size listed is about 100 calories.

The Healthy Carb Connection

The foods in the following table are some good choices of complex carbs. All are lower-glycemic choices, low in sugar, and minimally processed. All of the given serving sizes are 100 calories.

Carbohydrate Type	Food	Serving Size
Cereal/grain	Barley	½ cup cooked
Cereal/grain	Cereal (high fiber/no sugar), e.g., bran flakes	¾ cup
Cereal/grain	Lentils	½ cup cooked
Cereal/grain	Oatmeal (slow-cooked)	1 cup cooked
Cereal/grain	Rice (basmati/wild)	1 cup cooked

Cereal/grain	Rice (brown/whole grain)	1 cup cooked
Vegetables	Corn	3 tbsp./1 small ear
Vegetables	Garbanzo beans	¼ cup cooked
Vegetables	Peas	¾ cup cooked
Vegetables	Potato (brown/red)	1 small
Vegetables	Pumpkin	1 cup
Vegetables	Squash (all types)	1 cup
Vegetables	Yams (sweet potatoes)	1 small

Fruits are a great way to satisfy your sweet tooth and still stay true to your diet. They are generally high in fiber and packed with vitamins and other disease-fighting phytonutrients. All of the servings listed below are about 90 to 110 calories.

Carbohydrate Type	Food	Serving Size
Fruits	Apple	1 medium
Fruits	Apricots	4 small
Fruits	Berries (any)	1 cup
Fruits	Cherries	1 cup
Fruits	Grapefruit	½ medium
Fruits	Grapes	20 small
Fruits	Guava	1 medium
Fruits	Kiwifruit	1 medium
Fruits	Nectarine	1 medium
Fruits	Orange	1 small
Fruits	Peaches	3 small
Fruits	Pear	1 small
Fruits	Plums	3 small
Fruits	Prunes	8 small
Fruits	Strawberries	1½ cups

Free Vegetables

Think of the following vegetables as "free foods"—you can eat them as often as you like without having to worry about calories. Since they are all high in fiber and water and low in calories, they'll help you feel full throughout the day. They'll also slow down the absorption of fat and carbohydrates into the system and are all excellent for gastrointestinal health. Finally, they're all great sources of vitamins and minerals that are essential for good health.

Artichokes	Chives	Jicama	Spinach
Arugula	Collard greens	Kale	Sprouts
Asparagus	Cucumber	Kelp	Swiss chard
Bamboo shoots	Eggplant	Lettuce	Tomatoes
Bok choy	Endive	Mushrooms	Turnips
Broccoli	Fenugreek	Onions	Water chestnuts
Brussels sprouts	Garlic	Peppers	Watercress
Cabbage	Ginger	Radishes	Wheatgrass/juice
Cauliflower	Green beans	Rhubarb	Zucchini
Celery	Herbs	Rutabaga	
Chicory	Horseradish	Scallions	

Protein Power

All of the following foods are good choices of high-quality protein and are low in saturated fat. Although the meat proteins contain cholesterol, they're fairly lean, so there's not a lot of fat in each serving. Note that each serving size is about 100 calories.

Protein Type	Food	Serving Size
Dairy	Cottage cheese, fat-free	½ cup
Dairy/vegetable	Soy burger, fat-free	1 medium patty
Dairy/vegetable	Tofu, low-fat, low-sodium	½ cup
Dairy/vegetable	Veggie burger	1 medium patty
Dairy/vegetable	Veggie hot dog	1 large
Fish/seafood	Albacore tuna	3 oz. can
Fish/seafood	Crab meat	1 cup
Fish/seafood	Fish, pink (tuna/salmon/trout)	4 oz. cooked
Fish/seafood	Fish, white (sea bass, halibut)	4 oz. cooked
Fish/seafood	Salmon, canned in water, low-sodium	3 oz. can

Poultry	Chicken breast, skinless	3 oz. cooked
Poultry	Chicken dark meat, skinless	3 oz. cooked
Poultry	Egg	1 large
Poultry	Egg Beaters	4 oz. (½ cup)
Poultry	Egg whites	5 medium
Poultry	Turkey, ground, 97% lean	5 tbsp.
Poultry	Turkey, white meat, sliced, fat-free	3 slices
Poultry	Turkey breast, boneless, skinless	3 oz. cooked

One note about protein is that some foods, including chicken and red meat, take more effort for the body to digest. And the more work your body does during digestion, the more water it uses. That's why a diet that's high in protein can be dehydrating, so be sure to drink plenty of water (at least one liter), for each main meal, especially for those that are rich in protein.

Essential Fats

Fat gets a bad rap. Not all fat choices are bad. In fact, healthful fats go a long way in giving your food flavor, keeping you full longer, and helping you stick to your diet in the long run. The key is to choose healthful, monounsaturated fats (including those found in olive oil or avocados), rather than saturated fats

DO YOU HAVE A FOOD SENSITIVITY?

In a perfect world, you'd never feel ill. But sometimes an illness can be your body's way of telling you that something is not right. If your body is having trouble digesting certain foods, you may have a sensitivity to them and will probably be better off avoiding them entirely or minimizing them in your diet. Here are some signals to look for when it comes to food sensitivity. Pay attention to your foods or meals when you have the following reactions:

- Feeling tired
- Feeling energized
- Crampy feeling
- Gassiness or bloated feeling
- Indigestion or stomach pain
- Diarrhea
- Irritation of the skin

(found in animal foods like whole milk and bacon). Also try to avoid trans-fatty acids, which are added to foods like french fries and commercial baked goods, as well as margarines, crackers, candy, and other processed foods. These types of fats go undetected in the system and are not easily broken down; they have been shown to raise levels of LDL (the "bad" cholesterol) and are linked to certain ailments like heart disease. Choose from the following unsaturated fats, which are in serving sizes of about 100 calories.

Fat Type	Food	Serving Size
Vegetables	Avocado	½ small
Vegetables	Guacamole	4 tbsp.
Vegetables	Hummus	2 tbsp.
Vegetables	Nut butters: almond, cashew, etc.	1 tbsp.
Vegetables	Nuts: macadamias or almonds	⅓ cup
Vegetables	Nuts: peanuts, cashews, mixed	⅛ cup
Vegetables	Nuts: pecans or pistachios	¼ cup
Vegetables	Oil: olive, canola, flaxseed, sesame, or soybean	2 tsp.
Vegetables	Oil: corn, peanut, or sunflower	2 tsp.
Vegetables	Olives	4 medium
Vegetables	Peanut butter, natural, light (no added oil)	1 tbsp.
Vegetables	Sesame seeds	1 oz.
Vegetables	Sunflower seeds	2 oz.

THE A-LIST WEIGHT LOSS MEAL PLAN

To lose an average of one pound a week—which most experts say is a healthy average for dieters—you need to have a net loss of 3,500 calories. That's the number of calories that the body uses to support one pound. On a daily basis, that means you need to have a net loss of 500 calories. You can achieve this through diet, exercise, or a combination of both. If you want to lose weight without feeling deprived, shoot for a combination of 250 calories burned through exercise and cut another 250 calories a day in your diet. Many of the A-List Workout plans burn at least 250 calories (based on a 150-pound person—if you weigh more, you'll burn more calories; if you weigh less, you'll burn fewer).

Kick-start your A-List weight loss plan by doing the prescribed exercises in Chapter 5 and by following the 1,500-calorie-a-day meal plan for the first seven days of your program. This should be enough calories to help you meet your nutritional needs and still lose weight. The A-List weight loss workout actually burns nearly 400 calories a day on average, so you may find yourself needing a few additional snacks to stay satiated.

You can either repeat the diet, switching things around for the entire twelve-week plan, or begin substituting some of the foods listed on the previous pages. If you are still not feeling satisfied with the portions given, you may simply need a few more calories to meet your daily needs. If you are losing more than three pounds a week, increase your intake by 350 calories a day. If you're already at your goal weight, increase your intake by 500 calories.

Also, remember that the following meals are only a guideline to healthy eating. If you don't have access to some of the ingredients or dislike a certain food, feel free to make a substitution, using the foods listed in the preceding pages. Steer clear of fatty meats and highly processed canned or boxed items in favor of lean cuts, poultry, fresh fish, and plenty of fruits and vegetables. For beverages, try to stick to plain water whenever possible or light, unsweetened tea.

SEVEN-DAY MEAL PLAN

DAY 1

BREAKFAST
Cooked Oatmeal, page 206

SNACK
1 medium orange

LUNCH
Chicken Salad, page 207
3–4 small olives

Free vegetables for the day: broccoli, lettuce, tomato, cucumber

SNACK
Protein Shake, page 208

DINNER
Salmon on Basmati Rice, page 208
5 medium spears asparagus

DAY 2

BREAKFAST
Spinach and Feta Cheese Omelet,
page 209

SNACK
1 medium-sized peach

LUNCH
Tuna Salad with Avocado, page 209

SNACK
Protein Shake, page 208

DINNER
6 ounces chicken breast
2 teaspoons olive oil to grill chicken
breast
1 small sweet potato
Free vegetables for the day: asparagus,
cucumber, spinach, and squash
Add sprinkle of vinegar or lemon juice on
vegetables to taste.

DAY 3

BREAKFAST
Swiss Muesli, page 210, made with
blueberries

SNACK
1 cup strawberries

LUNCH
5 ounces lean beef or veggie burger
1 small seven-grain bun

Lettuce and tomato; use ketchup
sparingly

SNACK
Protein Shake, page 208

DINNER
Stir-Fried Tofu and Couscous, page 210

DAY 4

BREAKFAST
Cooked Oatmeal, page 206

SNACK
1 cup applesauce

LUNCH
1 cut roll (6 pieces) any type of sushi
1 cup miso soup
½ cup edamame (soybeans)
Mixed field greens, tomato

SNACK
Protein Shake, page 208, made with ¼
small banana

DINNER
Turkey Meatballs and Butternut Squash,
page 211
½ small avocado

DAY 5

BREAKFAST
1 cup All-Bran cereal (Any bran cereal will
do, but choose one that's low in sugar.)
1 cup nonfat or unsweetened soy milk

SNACK

1 apple

LUNCH

2 slices low-carb bread

2 teaspoons natural peanut butter

2 teaspoons natural jam

SNACK

Protein Shake, page 208

DINNER

Halibut on Basmati Rice, page 211

Free vegetables: cabbage, cauliflower, peppers, tomato

DAY 6

BREAKFAST

1 egg + 2 egg whites, any style

1 teaspoon olive oil

1 ounce cheese

Any vegetables can be added.

SNACK

1 cup fruit salad

LUNCH

1 medium low-carb tortilla

¼ cup mixed beans and rice

3 ounces grilled chicken

SNACK

Protein Shake, page 208

DINNER

Blackened Snapper on Brown Rice, page 212

Free veggies for the day: broccoli, spinach, mushrooms

DAY 7

BREAKFAST

Cooked Oatmeal, page 206

SNACK

2 plums

LUNCH

2 small veggie hot dogs

1 small potato

Mushrooms, red peppers, onions

SNACK

Protein Shake, page 208

DINNER

Barbecued Salmon on Brown Rice, page 212

Free veggies for the day: broccoli, onions, peppers

★ TIP: Follow the rainbow. Try to eat the colors of the rainbow every day, with at least two servings of fruits and three servings of vegetables. For example, choose tomatoes (red), tangerines (orange), peppers (green, red, or yellow), celery (green), carrots (orange), blueberries (blue), eggplant (purple), and zucchini (yellow or green). These foods are rich in vitamins and other antioxidants to help keep you healthy.

RECIPES FOR THE SEVEN-DAY MEAL PLAN

 COOKED OATMEAL

CALORIES: Approximately 200–250 | SERVINGS: 1 | PREP TIME: 5 minutes

INGREDIENTS:

1 cup oatmeal (instant or old-fashioned)

1 teaspoon essential fatty acid (See note.)

1 teaspoon plain soy or whey protein powder

TO PREPARE:

- If using instant oatmeal, place 1 cup oatmeal in a bowl, add hot water, and microwave on High for 1 minute.
- With old-fashioned oats, cook in a pot on the stovetop. Bring to a boil, and then reduce heat to low. Stir oatmeal continuously, and add a dash of salt to prevent sticking.
- When done, add the essential fatty acid.
- Add protein powder to the oatmeal slowly to avoid coagulation.

NOTE: Essential fatty acids (EFA) are a combination of healthy oils such as omega-3, omega-6, and flaxseed oil and can be found at most health food stores. Omega-3 EFA should be kept cold.

⭐ **TIP:** The best time to fuel up before exercising is about one to one and a half hours in advance of your workout. Choose a carbohydrate-rich option with a little bit of fat and protein for sustained energy, such as peanut butter on a slice of rye bread or a protein shake made with fresh raspberries. After exercising, you'll need a food that's about 60 percent carbohydrates and 40 percent protein, such as an energy shake and some fruit. You'll replenish your fuel stores more quickly and help your body get ready for its next workout.

CHICKEN SALAD

CALORIES: 250–300 | SERVINGS: 1 | PREP TIME: 25 minutes (plus 2 hours marinating time)

INGREDIENTS:

Dressing and Marinade

2 teaspoons olive oil

2 teaspoons balsamic vinegar

2 teaspoons lemon juice

¼ teaspoon crushed garlic

Dash black pepper

Dash cayenne pepper

Dash salt

2 teaspoons chopped fresh cilantro

Salad

5 ounces boneless, skinless chicken breast

1 small sweet potato

1 serving salad greens

1 tomato, sliced

2 hearts of palm

TO PREPARE:

- Combine oil, vinegar, lemon juice, garlic, black pepper, cayenne pepper, salt, and cilantro. Set aside 2–3 teaspoons to use as salad dressing.
- Marinate chicken breast in remaining dressing/marinade for 2 hours. Remove from mari-nade. Grill on an open flame or broil in the oven.
- Microwave sweet potato on High for 5 minutes, or until soft.
- Slice chicken into strips.
- Place chicken on a bed of mixed greens, tomato, and hearts of palm. Serve sweet potato on the side.

★ PROTEIN SHAKE

CALORIES: 200–250 | SERVINGS: 1 | PREP TIME: 5 minutes

INGREDIENTS:

6 ounces water

6 ounces soy milk

2 scoops protein powder

¼ small banana (optional)

¼ cup crushed ice

½ cup fruit: strawberries, blueberries, raspberries, bananas, or any fruit of your choice

TO PREPARE:

- In a blender, blend together water, soy milk, and protein powder.
- Add fruit and crushed ice; blend until smooth.

★ SALMON ON BASMATI RICE

CALORIES: 350 | SERVINGS: 1 | PREP TIME: 35 minutes (plus 2 hours marinating time)

INGREDIENTS:

1 teaspoon lemon juice

2 teaspoons balsamic vinegar

Dash soy sauce

Dash Worcestershire sauce

5-ounce salmon fillet

1 teaspoon olive oil

¼ cup uncooked basmati rice

TO PREPARE:

- Prepare rice per package instructions.
- Mix together lemon juice, balsamic vinegar, soy sauce, and Worcestershire sauce. Place salmon in mixture, and marinate for approximately 2 hours.
- Heat olive oil in a skillet over medium heat.
- Place salmon in skillet, sear both sides, and cook lightly or thoroughly, depending on your preference.
- Serve fish on a bed of basmati rice.

> ★ TIP: Drink early, drink often! Drinking a glass of water first thing in the morning will clear your digestive system to make way for nutrient transport. And remember to stay hydrated throughout the day. Drink often, even if it's just taking little sips all day long. This goes double for warm days and days when you're exercising more intensely, when your body's hydration needs become even more important.

SPINACH AND FETA CHEESE OMELET

CALORIES: 300 | SERVINGS: 1 | PREP TIME: 12 minutes

INGREDIENTS:

2 eggs

½ cup fresh spinach

1 ounce feta cheese

1 sprig fresh basil

1 slice whole-wheat bread

TO PREPARE:

- Whisk eggs thoroughly.
- Spray a nonstick pan with olive oil cooking spray, and heat on medium.
- Add egg to pan; cook 1 to 2 minutes.
- Before egg is fully set, add spinach, cheese, and basil. Toast bread.
- Fold egg in half, and serve with toast.

 TUNA SALAD WITH AVOCADO

CALORIES: 300 | SERVINGS: 1 | PREP TIME: 20 minutes

INGREDIENTS:

4 ounces canned tuna in water

1 teaspoon olive oil

1 serving mixed greens

1 tomato, chopped

2 pieces of hearts of palm (canned)

¼ avocado, sliced

¼ red bell pepper, sliced

½ cup kidney beans

Dressing

1 teaspoon mayonnaise

¼ teaspoon hot sauce

1 teaspoon lemon juice

Dash black pepper

TO PREPARE:

- Sauté tuna in oil in a nonstick pan for 5 minutes; place on mixed greens.
- In a bowl, combine tomato, hearts of palm, avocado, bell pepper, and kidney beans. Place vegetable mixture on top of tuna.
- Prepare dressing by placing ¼ cup boiling water in a heat-resistant glass. Add mayonnaise, hot sauce, lemon juice, and black pepper. Mix thoroughly, and pour over tuna salad.

★ SWISS MUESLI

| CALORIES: 300 | SERVINGS: 1 | PREP TIME: 10 minutes (plus 6–12 hours refrigeration) |

INGREDIENTS:

1 cup instant oatmeal

1 scoop protein powder

1 cup soy milk (divided into ½-cup portions)

¼ cup low-fat or fat-free yogurt

¼ cup blueberries or other berries

TO PREPARE:

- Place oatmeal in a bowl, add protein powder, and mix with a spoon.
- Add ½ cup soy milk and the yogurt and berries; mix thoroughly.
- Refrigerate overnight to let ingredients mix well.
- Add remaining ½ cup soy milk, and serve.

★ STIR-FRIED TOFU AND COUSCOUS

| CALORIES: 250 | SERVINGS: 1 | PREP TIME: 25 minutes |

INGREDIENTS:

¾ cup uncooked couscous

½ medium onion

1 tablespoon olive oil

1 sprig rosemary

Pinch oregano

1 teaspoon minced garlic

½ red bell pepper, chopped

1 zucchini, sliced

½ tomato, chopped

1 cup sliced mushrooms

5 ounces firm tofu

1 teaspoon curry powder

1 bay leaf

TO PREPARE:

- Prepare couscous according to package directions.
- Sauté ½ onion in olive oil with rosemary, oregano, and garlic.
- Add bell pepper and zucchini; stir-fry about 3 to 5 minutes.
- Add tomato and mushrooms; cook 1 to 2 minutes.
- Add tofu, curry, and bay leaf; simmer 5 minutes.
- Serve stir-fry over couscous.

TURKEY MEATBALLS AND BUTTERNUT SQUASH

CALORIES: 350 | SERVINGS: 1 | PREP TIME: 1 hour

INGREDIENTS:

1 small butternut squash

½ cup (about 4 ounces) ground turkey

¼ small onion, chopped

¼ red bell pepper, chopped

¼ teaspoon minced garlic

1 teaspoon lemon juice

¼ teaspoon dried parsley

¼ cup frozen green peas

1 tablespoon olive oil

TO PREPARE:

■ Cut butternut squash in half, lengthwise. Place half of squash faceup on baking sheet, and bake in oven at 300°F for 1 hour; allow to cool.

■ While squash is baking, combine turkey, onion, bell pepper, garlic, lemon juice, parsley, and peas in a medium bowl. Mix thoroughly in a food processor or blender.

■ Roll mixture into small meatballs. Heat oil in a nonstick pan over medium heat; add meatballs. Sauté, turning occasionally, until cooked thoroughly.

■ Serve meatballs with squash.

HALIBUT ON BASMATI RICE

CALORIES: 350 | SERVINGS: 1 | PREP TIME: 30 minutes

INGREDIENTS:

¼ cup uncooked basmati rice

Dash paprika

Dash onion salt

Dash garlic powder

Dash cayenne pepper

½ lemon

5 ounces halibut

TO PREPARE:

■ Prepare grill. Cook basmati rice according to package instructions.

■ Mix together paprika, onion salt, garlic powder, and cayenne pepper; add juice from lemon. Dip halibut into mixture.

■ Grill fish approximately 7 to 10 minutes per side on medium heat; serve over rice.

BLACKENED SNAPPER ON BROWN RICE

CALORIES: 250 | SERVINGS: 1 | PREP TIME: 25 minutes

INGREDIENTS:

¼ cup uncooked brown rice

1 teaspoon Cajun spice

Dash cayenne pepper

½ teaspoon crushed bay leaf

1 teaspoon salt

½ teaspoon cinnamon

½ teaspoon crushed oregano

¼ teaspoon paprika

Juice of 1 lemon

5 ounces red snapper

2 teaspoons olive oil

TO PREPARE:

- Prepare rice as per box directions
- Mix Cajun spice, cayenne pepper, bay leaf, salt, cinnamon, oregano, and paprika in a small bowl.
- Squeeze lemon juice over fish.
- Press spice mixture onto fish.
- Heat skillet on high; add olive oil.
- Sauté fish on hot skillet for 5 to 7 minutes.
- Serve on a bed of brown rice.

> ★ TIP: Be preemptive. If you are going out to eat, visiting friends, or taking part in any other social occasion that you know might be difficult for your diet, have a light meal or healthful snack before you go. You'll be less likely to binge on the fattening choices that will face you.

 ## BARBECUED SALMON ON BROWN RICE

CALORIES: 300–350 | SERVINGS: 1 | PREP TIME: 30 minutes

INGREDIENTS:

¼ cup uncooked brown rice

5 ounces salmon

2 tablespoons barbecue sauce

TO PREPARE:

- Prepare grill or broiler. Cook brown rice according to package instructions.
- Dip salmon in barbecue sauce to glaze.
- Place salmon on barbecue or broiler, and cook at high heat until done.
- Serve salmon over cooked rice.

The following recipes can be substituted for those listed in the Seven-Day Meal Plan.

CHICKEN AND VEGGIE SKEWERS

CALORIES: 250 | SERVINGS: 1 | PREP TIME: 30 minutes

INGREDIENTS:

1 medium potato, peeled and cubed

6 mushrooms, cut into chunks

1 green or red bell pepper, sliced

6 small pieces of broccoli

6 ounces boneless, skinless chicken breast, cubed

Dash garlic powder

Dash salt

Dash black pepper

Dash poultry seasoning

2 sprigs fresh rosemary

TO PREPARE:

- Prepare grill or broiler. Parboil potato for 10 minutes.
- On a wooden skewer, thread mushrooms, bell pepper, broccoli, chicken, and potato.
- Combine garlic powder, salt, black pepper, and poultry seasoning in a small bowl. Rub spice mixture on skewered chicken and vegetables.
- Cook on an open-flame grill or under broiler for 20 to 30 minutes, turning several times.
- Serve with fresh rosemary for garnish.

★ TIP: Prevent dehydration. All cells in the body require hydration, so it's extremely important to drink plenty of water and eat hydrating foods like fruits and vegetables, especially when it comes to maintaining a high metabolism. Coffee, sodas, other caffeinated beverages, and alcohol are all diuretics, which means the body will flush them out. Keep these choices to a minimum, say, no more than one cup of coffee or black tea a day.

★ COBB SALAD

CALORIES: 250 | SERVINGS: 1 | PREP TIME: 10 minutes

INGREDIENTS:

¼ head romaine lettuce

1 tomato, diced

2 artichoke hearts, sliced

¼ avocado, sliced

3 olives, cut into fourths

1 hardboiled egg, sliced

2 teaspoons olive oil

2 teaspoons balsamic vinegar

TO PREPARE:

- In a bowl, combine lettuce, tomato, artichokes, avocado, olives, and egg.
- Sprinkle with oil and vinegar for dressing.

★ GRILLED TOFU SALAD

CALORIES: 250 | SERVINGS: 1 | PREP TIME: 10 minutes (plus 1 hour marinating time)

INGREDIENTS:

2 tablespoons orange juice

1 tablespoon teriyaki sauce

5 ounces firm tofu

1 cup mixed greens

1 tomato

¼ onion, sliced

6 mushrooms, sliced

1 artichoke heart, chopped

2 spears asparagus, steamed

2 teaspoons olive oil

2 teaspoons balsamic vinegar

TO PREPARE:

- Combine orange juice and teriyaki sauce to make a marinade. Cut tofu into chunks, and marinate for at least 1 hour. Remove from marinade, and stir-fry 3 to 5 minutes.
- Place tofu on a bed of mixed greens. Add tomato, onion, mushrooms, artichoke heart, and asparagus.
- Drizzle with oil and vinegar for dressing.

★ **TIP:** Whenever you can, avoid processed foods, sweeteners, additives, and preservatives. The more the food is in its natural state, the easier it will be for your body to digest. Unprocessed foods also tend to be higher in fiber and have fewer calories, so they'll fill you up, take longer to break down, and keep you energized.

Resources

THE TRAINERS IN THIS BOOK all have their own very fine workout programs and products, from books and videos to Podcasts and other downloadable routines. You can also reach many through their own websites.

TRAINER INFORMATION

Mike Alexander
Madfitness.com

Teddy Bass
Premier trainer, podfitness.com
Teddybass.com

Ashley Borden
Premier trainer, podfitness.com
ashleyborden.com

Joe Dowdell
Owner, Peak Performance Strength & Conditioning Center
Peakperformancenyc.com
Author, *The Model You*

Rich Edward Guzmán and Helene Chimbidis Guzmán
Co-owners, LARox Fitness
Premier trainers, podfitness.com
larox.net

Jeanette Jenkins
Creator of seven DVDs: *The Hollywood Trainer Ab Blast, Kickboxing Boot-camp, Cardio Sculpt, Butt and Thigh Blast, Pilates, Yoga, Ultimate Cross Training*
Author, *The Hollywood Trainer Weight-Loss Plan* (Putnam, 2007)
Premier trainer, podfitness.com
thehollywoodtrainer.com

Larry Krug
Founder, Eatwize Lifestyle and Nutrition
eatwize.com

Gunnar Peterson
Creator, Core Secrets, eighteen functional training and core strength workout DVDs/videotapes
Author, *The Workout* (HarperCollins, 2006)
gunnarpeterson.com; coresecrets.com

Christel Smith
mindbodymiracles.com

EQUIPMENT

For the workout gear and equipment such as the resistance bands, medicine balls, stability balls, and dumbbells featured in this book, contact Perform Better.com.

For dumbbells, strength benches, and other strength-training equipment, contact Fitness EM at fitnessem.com.

For the fitness apparel that appears in some of the chapters, contact Champion Apparel at championcatalog.com.

Index

Page numbers in *italics* refer to recipes.